PRINCESS ANNE

A royal girl of our time

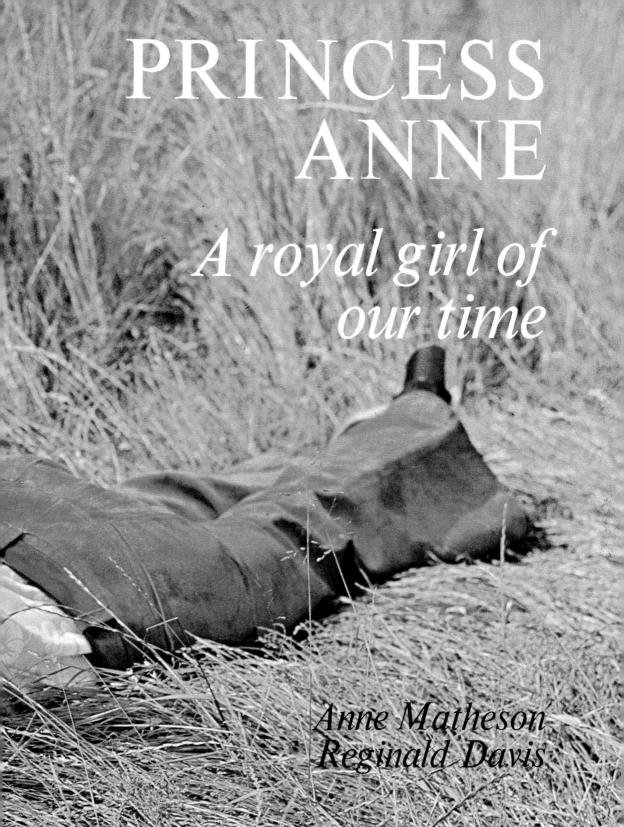

PRINCESS ANNE

*A royal girl of
our time*

*Anne Matheson
Reginald Davis*

CROWN PUBLISHERS, INC., NEW YORK

Published in the U.S.A. by Crown Publishers, Inc.

ISBN: 0 517 513986

Contents

Introduction

The marriage of Her Royal Highness Princess Anne to Captain Mark Phillips is the fifth Royal Wedding I have attended since, on 20 November, 1947, on a bleak late autumn day twenty-six years ago, I went to Westminster Abbey to report the wedding of her mother.

Princess Elizabeth, heir presumptive to the Throne, was marrying the youthful, blonde and handsome former Lieutenant Philip Mountbatten, Royal Navy, one time Prince of the Royal House of Greece. But on that morning a new title had been conferred on him by King George VI. He was now His Royal Highness Prince Philip, Duke of Edinburgh, Earl of Merioneth, Baron Greenwich of Greenwich in the County of London and a Knight Commander of the Most Noble Order of the Bath, all this happily linking Scotland,

7

Wales and the tradition of the British Navy.

The wedding of Elizabeth and Philip held particular meaning for the English people in that it was the first post-war occasion which gave the country back something of its traditional pomp. By an overwhelming majority of eighty-six per cent, people had voted to do away with austerity. 'Let us make a day of it she and all of us will remember' was the popular verdict.

The U.S. news magazine *Time* reported that 'Austerity, coal crises, rationing and shortages faded from the news columns to make way for reports of the lovers'. In those bleak days the British realised how sadly they had felt the lack of colour in their lives. The Royal wedding, as if by a miracle, gave them back the colour and pageantry of the nation's history. Instead of probing television cameras, my impressions had to supply a good deal of the colour: the scarlet and gold uniforms of the Yeomen of the Guard, the richness of the embroideries and vestments of the clergy, the red cassocks of the choir boys of the Chapels Royal, the gay mosaic of hats and dresses of the two-thousand guests in the crowded nave and transepts awaiting the arrival of the bride. The high altar, hung with embroideries and fine lace, flanked by massive alabaster vases filled with lovely flowers. The rich glow of the Abbey gold plate.

All this, right to the last notes of the wedding march and the dying echoes of the trumpets as they were lost in the gothic traceries of the Abbey roof, comes back vividly to me in memory as the whole scene is re-enacted once more with Princess Anne as the young and beautiful bride. Twice already I have seen Princess Anne as part of this Royal wedding pageantry in Westminster Abbey – when she was a bridesmaid to her aunt Princess Margaret and again to her cousin Princess Alexandra. Also I saw her as bridesmaid to Miss Katherine Worsley when she married the Duke of Kent in majestic York Minster, a marriage solemnised by Dr. A. M. Ramsay, then Archbishop of York, now the Archbishop of Canterbury and, as such, officiating at Princess Anne's own wedding in Westminster Abbey.

Each time, as I watched Princess Anne, the thought has been in my mind that it would not be too many years before she would, herself, be a radiant bride.

So while the wedding of Anne and Mark is a splendid public occasion it is also very much a family affair. And it would be impossible for me to view it entirely from the professional journalistic angle. I was, after all, the first person in the world to drop a curtsy to the Queen of England, Elizabeth the Second. On the morning she descended from Treetops, where she had kept a night-long vigil on the prowling wild animals of Kenya at a waterhole beneath, I was waiting to collect my material for a story on this part of her tour. In the cool of the early morning Elizabeth gave me a bright and happy smile as she drove off.

But during the night King George VI had died, although the news did not reach us in that remote corner of the world until some hours later. Elizabeth, in fact, succeeded to the Throne while sitting in a simple construction of rest rooms built on a plank across the spreading branches of a large tree.

I was to see this young Queen bring up her children with all the care of a devoted mother, in spite of her formidable official life and awesome responsibilities.

Although I have known Princess Anne since she was a baby, watched her grow up, met her frequently at parties at Buckingham Palace, on board the Royal Yacht *Britannia*, in the stately ballrooms of the Queen's representatives in Commonwealth countries, as well as informally on safari, in the Australian outback, by the lonely atolls of the Pacific, this can be no more than a sketch of the Princess.

As she approached marriage Princess Anne was only just 23, and although she had packed much action into these years one hopes for her that many more lie ahead for useful fulfillment of her ideals and pursuits. She has accomplished much already that gives a firm pointer to a future that biographers will be proud to record.

Anne is the first Princess in a thousand years of British Monarchy to have been allowed to grow up with the freedom to live her own life. She has become very much a Princess of our times, and has helped the Monarchy to move closer to the people without losing its dignity and mystique. Princess Anne's freedom means not an arranged marriage but one to the man of her choice, riding to championship class and a world title, dressing much the same as other girls of her age from inexpensive off-the-peg ranges – even her wedding dress was made by a ready-to-wear firm specially for the day.

Introduction

She enjoys the simple as well as the sophisticated pleasures of the world around her. She likes dining out where the menu is uncomplicated but the company is rich, loves dancing and discotheques, enjoys fast driving and taking photographs and prefers pop to classical music. Yet, all the time she remains very much a Princess who works hard and gives the Queen tremendous support and the Monarchy the little extra boost that comes from having a bright new star in its heavens.

She has grown up with young people. As well as elder brother Charles, she has two younger brothers, Prince Andrew and Prince Edward, and young cousins all of whom adore the boisterous, fun-loving Anne. She goes racing with them in Go-Karts, at breakneck speeds down the sharply twisting paths from Balmoral Castle to the stables. There are shrieks of delight from Lady Sarah Armstrong-Jones as, seated between Princess Anne's knees, they take turns at speed, enveloping everyone in dust.

But Anne knows that not all children are so fortunate in life, and she treats them all as equals. I have seen how quickly Anne can turn any child's world into a brighter place.

After her engagement was announced and the family was finishing the celebration luncheon at Buckingham Palace, Princess Anne excused herself and went off in a helicopter because she had an important date – with a group of disabled children she had done much to help to a new way of life at a riding school planned specially for them.

11

Anne in Love

It was with a smile on her face but a sorely troubled heart that Princess Anne left London in February, 1973, for a twelve-day visit to Ethiopia.

Even the happiest married couples looking back agree there is no denying the old saying, 'The course of true love never did run smooth.' For a Royal Princess it is an even more sober reality. Anne had had little or no privacy in the early days of her romance with Lieutenant Mark Phillips. The strength of the British monarchy depends to a great extent on the spotlight of publicity; preferably on its own terms, of course. And Princess Anne had had it unremittingly and blindingly focused on Mark and herself at the very time when their growing fondness for each other was still unresolved.

There was little doubt in Princess Anne's own mind

that Mark Phillips was the only man with whom she felt she could spend the rest of her life. She felt sure but, partly because she herself is a strong, positive character and partly because of the seriousness with which marriage must be regarded in the Royal family, she had to be very sure.

Not that things weren't going well. The Queen liked Mark. But she wanted to get to know him better than as Mark Phillips, the outstanding horseman, so he was invited to spend the New Year with the Royal family at Sandringham.

Sandringham is the Queen's private home where there is none of the formality of the official Royal residences. It is a pleasant house set in a 20,000-acre estate which the Royal family have owned for more than a century. The house is tastefully furnished with vast log fires and guest rooms always prepared. It is a typical English country house, and welcoming.

The Queen is always happy at Sandringham, affectionately known in the family as the Big House. Here they were all to get to know Mark Phillips. At the end of his visit, had there been any doubt about whether he would fit into the patterns of the Royal way of life, he would not have been asked again.

One of Princess Margaret's first young men was invited to Sandringham to a weekend house party. When asked by the Queen Mother why he had not joined them for church on Sunday he replied casually, 'Oh, I usually sleep in on Sunday morning.' Later he said, 'I found myself quietly frozen out.'

14

1973 B.A.O.
Horse Trials
Bad Lippspring
West German

Mark Phillips, however, was invited again the following weekend. This did not mean that a 'marriage had been arranged'. By the standards of the Queen and Prince Philip, whose love grew over many years and out of childhood friendship, the romance of Anne and Mark was sudden. The Queen gave her daughter a hint that she realised how serious things were becoming but she handled the delicate matter with a tactful touch of lightness. 'Don't rush your fences,' she counselled her daughter.

Young Lieutenant Phillips, too, wanted time to think things out. He felt sure of his love for Princess Anne but he had to come to terms with himself and her Royal position.

So the good-bye kisses after the Sandringham visits at the Harwich dockside, where he rejoined his unit for the night crossing to Germany, were lightly exchanged.

The romance was still only a matter of some months old. Although, looking back now, every lover of Royal romance is as sure as Anne and Mark how and where it all began. The date: September 3, 1972; the place: a discotheque in Munich. A note, hand-written, was sent by Princess Anne to a young reporter on the social pages of a leading Munich paper. The reporter had sent a note asking the Princess' permission to take photographs. Anne's note said: 'The simple answer is NO. I'm sorry, but that's final. I'd be grateful if you complied. It is a private party.'

Disconsolately the photographer left, but the young

16

reporter, dressed up for what she had hoped was a meeting with the Princess, decided to make a night of it, and stayed on to see the very beginnings of a romance that was to have a very happy ending.

The party in the discotheque was to celebrate Britain's two Golds at the Munich Olympics: the Three-Day Event, which they had also won at the Olympics in Mexico, and Richard Meade's individual Gold.

Mark Phillips, who was in the British Three-Day Event team with Mary Gordon-Watson and Bridget Parker, led by 33-year-old Meade, was there too.

The hero of the evening was Richard Meade, the team leader and the first British rider to win the individual Gold at the Olympics.

Princess Anne had been giving the British team her full support, though there was more than a touch of poignancy. If it hadn't been for the injury of her horse Doublet she might have been part of the Olympic team. Instead she watched the competitors through her binoculars and, as Richard Meade came close to where she was sitting, she would pick up her camera and begin snapping.

And she was one of the first to congratulate him. Rushing down from the stand, leaving Special Branch men trailing behind her, to find the other British team members excited and emotional but Richard cool and relaxed, letting the strain of the contest drain out of him. 'This must be the greatest day of my life,' he told her.

But in the discotheque the Princess took hardly any

notice of the rider everyone expected to find her hero-worshipping all evening, but danced the night away with another young man. What was his name? Lieutenant Mark Phillips. Those interested enough could find it on the Olympic programme.

The discotheque in Munich is probably as close as anyone could get to saying where it all began. But 'How does anything start?' Mark Phillips says in reply to the question.

But where would it end? In happy marriage? Or would it shrivel in the bright glare of premature publicity? Winging her way across Africa to the ancient, romantic kingdom of Ethiopia, Anne pondered her future.

The trip to Ethiopia offered everything to appeal to her sense of fun and adventure and the time spent in the

1973 Badminton Horse Trials. Mark Phillip's father on the left wearing a trilby

exotic setting probably did much to refresh her spirits and clear her mind.

She was fêted by the Emperor Haile Selassie, survived a three-day mule trek through some of the most rugged country in the world, photographed the rare ibex, barbecued on the very roof of Africa. And in the port of Massawa made a conquest of a Russian admiral. She tossed aside formalities and wore a Soviet sailor's hat on top of her own topee and joined wholeheartedly in the spirit of the welcome the Russians gave her.

Every experience was new and fascinating to her.

Princess Anne with the Royal Worcs. Regiment and the Sherwood Foresters in Berlin, June 1973

19

Though at times the heat, the flies, the dust and some-
times the fleas from the mangy lions at the court of the
King of Judah looked as though they would defeat her,
Princess Anne was never daunted.

Even when she had to leave a banqueting table in a
hurry for the ladies' room when she had a vomiting
attack she was back in less than an hour and cancelled
no more than half the next day's programme.

But if Mark Phillips was often on her mind he was
also on the minds of the press that covered the tour.

So in the middle of the tour Princess Anne issued another one of her famous denials: 'We are not engaged
and there is no prospect of an engagement.'

This statement was not for publication, only a direc-
tive for editors. And it was accompanied by the usual
explanation that they were only seen together because of
their mutual interest in horse riding and competition.

The journalists gathered in Addis Ababa were
astounded. The more optimistic of them had been
expecting Mark Phillips to fly out to join the Princess.
The tour wasn't yielding all that much copy and they
were hoping for a story they could get their teeth into.

The suspicion arose that Anne and Mark had had
some sort of a quarrel, that one of them had called the
whole thing off. But which one?

The wires to Lieutenant Phillips' quarters ran hot.
But never once did he betray the least surprise or
emotion, hurt or otherwise. He loyally backed Princess
Anne, confirming the story as she had told it.

But soon, and entirely because of Princess Anne's

own doing, there were ripples of speculation again on the waters she had sought to calm. No sooner had her plane touched down at London's Heathrow airport, at 7.30 a.m., than she stepped into her brand new Scimitar, waiting on the tarmac. Within half an hour she could have been having breakfast with the Queen and her father at Windsor Castle. Instead she put her foot down on the accelerator and was once again tearing along the M4 to Mark Phillips' house.

Before the photographers and speculation could catch up with them, they were out riding together.

If Anne and Mark had shared some other common interest, say, music or art, or even Prince Philip's absorption in conversation, it might have been possible to pursue their courtship in part indoors, or at least in quiet places. But competition riding inevitably took them where there were people and press. So one denial followed another.

It is amusing to look back on an entry in Queen Victoria's diary and see how in many senses life remains unchanging for the Royal family, even for such a girl of our times as Princess Anne. All members of the Royal family must keep a diary—as Prince Charles remarked wryly, 'Not to be read for a hundred years from now.' Queen Victoria's journal could set the scene for her great-great-great-granddaughter a hundred years later.

Extract from Victoria's journal:

'About 10 miles from Ballachulish . . . . 1873.

'We sat down on the grass (we three) on our plaids,

Anne in Love

and had our luncheon, served by Brown and Francie, and then I sketched. The day was most beautiful and calm. Here, however—here, in this complete solitude, we were spied upon by impudent, inquisitive reporters, who followed us everywhere; but one in particular (who writes for some of the Scotch papers) lay down and watched with a telescope and dodged me and Beatrice and Jane Churchill, who were walking about, and was most impertinent when Brown went to tell him to move, which Jane herself had thought of doing. However, he did go away at last, and Brown came back saying he thought there would have been a fight; for when Brown said, quite civilly, that the Queen wished him to move away, he said he had quite as good a right to remain there as the Queen. To this Brown answered very strongly, upon which the impertinent individual asked, "Did he know who he was?" and Brown answered that he did, and that "the highest gentleman in England would not dare do what he did, much less a reporter— and he must move on, or he would give him something more". And the man said, "Would he dare do that before those other men (all reporters) who were coming up". And Brown answered "Yes" he would before "anybody who did not behave as he thought fit." More strong words were used; but the others came up and advised the man to come away quietly, which he finally did.

'Such conduct ought to be known.'

That was in Victoria's day. In 1973 Anne was handling matters for herself.

Her next and most positive denial came at Warfield

23

op Left, *At Badminton with the Queen in 1960*
op Right, *Welcomed by her fiancé at Hanover airport, 1973*
ower Left, *By the lake in the grounds of Buckingham Palace, 1973*
ower Right, *On the Grand Staircase of Buckingham Palace, 1973*

in Berkshire, where she and Mark Phillips were training horses together, on 2 March.

Anne broke off from exercising horses in a field to make her statement to agency reporter Gillian Garner. Gillian Garner was standing with a photographer on a public footpath next to the field when Anne spotted them and rode over. She asked what they were doing. Gillian Garner said they were watching the jumping.

The conversation then reportedly went like this:

Anne: 'Haven't you ever seen anyone train horses before?'

Gillian: 'Yes, on many occasions.'

Anne: 'Did you ask anyone to confirm that it is a public footpath?'

Gillian: 'No, I did not. But if I were asked to go I would remove myself.'

Anne: 'Well, I might remove you. Which paper do you work for?'

Gillian: 'I work for an agency serving the nationals.'

Anne: 'Well, that sounds as if you are being deliberately evasive. What is the name of the agency?'

Gillian: 'The Southern News Service, which represents the national dailies.'

Anne: 'Thank you. I don't know what you people are doing here every day.'

Gillian: 'With respect, surely you must be aware of the speculation and rumour of romance between yourself and Lieutenant Phillips.'

Anne: 'There is no romance between us and there are no grounds for these rumours of a romance between us. He is here solely to exercise the horse he will be riding at Badminton.'

The conversation ended when Anne said, 'Here comes a friend of mine to talk to you.' As her private detective walked over, she rode off.

After the incident there was the usual reiteration of denials from Mark Phillips and from Buckingham Palace.

Two months later Anne and Mark were engaged. How did the British Press, which had been so convincingly led up the garden path by all concerned, forgive Anne? The press is strongly aware how much the Royal family depends on good relationships with newspapers, radio and television. Sometimes members of the Royal family—although the Queen never forgets her Royal decorum—play little games of hide and seek with the Press and the Press with them, but Princess Anne had deliberately lied about her situation.

One journalist summed it up: 'Heaven forbid the suggestion that Princess Anne was telling even the smallest white lie. But it does throw some light on the difficulties implicit in a Royal romance of the 1970s. Courting is for candlelight. Princess Anne got flashlight.'

In the months after the engagement, with marriage approaching, when the photographers began to get a series of tender and moving pictures of Anne and Mark they had their golden princess back again and she could do no wrong. Anne and Mark were so clearly in love. The British public rejoiced for them; the British press forgave them. Anne in love could do no wrong.

25

The courtship of Anne and Mark

The announcement of the engagement of Princess Anne, 22, and Lieutenant Mark Phillips, a 24-year-old officer serving with the Queen's Dragoon Guards came in a month of May that was anything but merry and to a Britain where few things seemed to be going right.

The Court Circular confirmed from Buckingham Palace, May 29: 'It is with the greatest pleasure that the Queen and the Duke of Edinburgh announce the betrothal of their beloved daughter the Princess Anne to Lieutenant Mark Phillips, the Queen's Dragoon Guards, son of Mr and Mrs Peter Phillips.'

On the British newspaper posters this was spelled out as 'ANNE AND MARK TO WED'. These wiped off the posters which for the past few weeks had proclaimed the latest details in the Lord-Lambton-and-the-call-girls affair, or

27

the squabbles in the boardrooms of Lonrho (in which Angus Ogilvy, husband of Princess Alexandra, would have been involved if he had not hastily resigned his seat) and the bedroom and boardroom behaviour of financier Bernie Cornfeld.

Here in a stroke was something to sweep away morbid fascination with the sleazy, the engagement of a young Royal princess and a soldier who was also a hero in the world of horsemanship. The British were happier than they had been for a long time. Happy for their Princess, and happy for themselves that, once more, the Monarchy had come to their rescue in the nick of time, and they could stand tall in the world again.

From Washington came a newspaper report of a woman who was getting ready for a garden party at the British Embassy. 'Thank God for Anne and her marvellous timing,' she is quoted as saying. 'It would have been a bit tricky chatting to all those Englishmen about their dreadful lords and all that call-girl business. But now we'll just talk about that wonderful little girl and that lovely man of hers.'

It is doubtful if anyone would accept that Anne and Mark became engaged to save a Washington hostess social embarrassment. It is absurd to carry this idea to its logical conclusion and suggest that the Queen and the Duke of Edinburgh were prepared to sacrifice the happiness of their only daughter in order to distract attention from a series of sordid scandals. But it is certainly true that some of the Queen's advisers and the

The courtship of Anne and Mark

British government must have felt that if Anne and Mark were lucky in having found their true love, the timing was equally lucky for the country.

Meanwhile, Mark was getting his first taste of life as a member of the British Royal family. In some ways the family life of the Queen mirrors exactly that of her subjects; in other ways it is irreconcilably different.

The family celebration at Balmoral was quiet over the long Whitsun weekend. Balmoral Castle was still dust-sheeted until the August holiday, which brings everyone together there, so the Queen and her family, and Mark, of course, stayed at the holiday house in the grounds called 'Craigowan'.

Princess Margaret, Lord Snowdon and their two children stayed with Queen Elizabeth the Queen Mother at nearby Birkhall. And to everyone's delight Prince Charles got sixty hours' shore leave and flew from St. Kitts in the Caribbean to join in the celebrations.

There can have been no happier gathering of the Royal family in recent years than this one. All the formalities were over: the Prime Minister, the Commonwealth Prime Ministers, the Archbishop of Canterbury, had been informed. Lieutenant Mark Phillips, although he claimed afterwards that he was 'petrified' of Prince Philip's reaction, had asked for Princess Anne's hand in marriage, so that he was able to begin to settle down to an easier relationship with his future father-in-law. 'He was very good to me,' Mark said later.

The family sat late over the celebration dinner, as families will when there is much to talk about.

'Craigowan' is too small to house the kind of staff it takes to run Buckingham Palace or Windsor Castle, so when the tables were cleared and the servants had gone to their homes on the estate, the family had the place to themselves. As May in Scotland is still a little chilly, they drew chairs around the fire and more or less made a night of it.

Dawn comes early at Balmoral in summer, as it is so far north. And it was soon after dawn that the family gathering broke up. Prince Charles left to rejoin his ship, which he caught up with in Antigua. Princess Margaret and Lord Snowdon left later with their children by plane for London. The Queen and Prince Philip, Princess Anne, Mark and two younger sons, Prince Andrew and Prince Edward, all came down from Aberdeen, making an overnight journey on the Royal train.

When the train reached London at eight o'clock there was a lively welcome from crowds who had got up early to greet the newly engaged couple.

This was a new experience for Mark Phillips, a foretaste of what his life will be. Mark Phillips is not unused to adulation. He has been twice a winner at Badminton and narrowly missed doing the hat trick there on his horse Great Ovation. He has European, World and Olympic Gold medals. He had also been given the highest accolade—to ride Columbus for the Queen. He had taken over the horse nine months before. It had proved too big and cussed for Princess Anne but he was realising its great potential.

But he had never had anything like the cheers that

greeted him when he stepped from the train with Princess Anne and his Labrador dog, Moriarty, and hers, Flora.

It was a boisterous and wholehearted welcome. Some wanted to see the Princess' ring. But most wanted to get a good look at Mark Phillips.

Few had seen the young lieutenant out of uniform and cap or dressed in riding rig. Now they saw a tall slender young man with fair-to-brown hair, a straight nose and good English features. He was tanned by the sun and his grin was wide. He had an easy, casual, assured air. Riding and army life keep him superbly fit and, despite his height of 6 feet $1\frac{1}{2}$ in., keeps his weight down to just under twelve stone.

The crowds liked what they saw.

Princess Anne had never looked happier. She was so relaxed and happy, so full of good humour that no one could have believed that this was the same girl who had got on her high horse to deny that there was any romance between her and Mark Phillips. She waved cheerfully to the crowds who stopped for a moment on their way to shops and offices. Mark, sitting beside her in the Rolls Royce, gave his first, stiff and self-conscious wave out of the other window.

The young lovers had a late breakfast at Buckingham Palace, then Princess Anne and Mark began to open the masses of telegrams of good wishes that had been piling up in her office, which is a small room in the Princess' suite set aside for her daily correspondence and used by her lady-in-waiting.

33

Later in the morning photographs of the newly engaged couple were taken in the grounds of the Palace, followed by one of those group pictures that appear in every family album.

Mark's parents, Mr and Mrs Peter Phillips, drove up from their home, a sixteenth-century farmhouse in Great Somerford, Wiltshire, where Princess Anne had been a welcome and frequent guest, in time for the photographic session and stayed for lunch.

It was in the Palace gardens that the true story of the romance began to unfold.

Princess Anne did most of the talking and spoke with engaging frankness about their engagement, which had been kept secret for five weeks. 'That was a bit of a strain,' she confessed. But it was Mark who pinpointed the actual date that the engagement began. 'It was after Badminton,' he said.

As one of their horsey friends quipped: 'Mark fell off his horse and on to his feet.'

It was in Mark's home village that the true-life romance unfolded in a way no fiction writer would have dared to write.

A generation before, the Queen, as Princess Elizabeth, made use of early morning rides with Princess Margaret over the high veldt in South Africa as an excuse to get to an isolated phone booth and a call from Prince Philip of Greece. And the Mayor of Capetown had a telephone installed in his parlour especially for that one call from London which would make the ball for Her Royal

Yellowknife, Northwest Territories, during the Royal Tour of Canada, July 1970

35

the grounds of Buckingham Palace, June 1973

Highness. And Princess Margaret went about with her photographer friend, Antony Armstrong-Jones, quite freely because she and her lady-in-waiting cleverly made use of wigs which became an almost perfect disguise.

But it took the wit and ingenuity of Princess Anne and Mark Phillips to put Her Royal Highness in a horse box and tow her around the countryside to a spot safe from prying eyes. But even after this brilliant stroke the young lovers needed many loyal accomplices and these were not lacking.

The most involved of these were undoubtedly Mark's own youthful-minded parents. Peter and Anne Phillips live at Mount House in the Wiltshire village of Great Somerford, which was pretty and well cared for enough to win the title 'Best Kept Village' before fame and tourists descended to litter the streets with rubbish and temporarily lose for this pleasant place its good name.

The Phillips' home of Cotswold stone and primrose wash is modest by Royal standards, but the kind of house which people, whatever their means, are finding far more comfortable to live in these days than country mansions that need a large staff to keep up.

Mark's father, Peter Phillips, was a major in the First Queen's Dragoon Guards, winning a Military Cross with the Eighth Army but later gave up his Army career for farming in Worcestershire. A motorway built closer to them than they cared for, drove the Phillips off their three hundred and sixty-six hard-worked acres at Long Green. Mark was nine years old when Peter and Anne Phillips moved to their present house of rural charm but little land, just enough to house the cluster of out-buildings, stables and loose boxes needed for the horses.

Mr Phillips joined the board of the big food processors, Walls, buying up pigs for sausage-making. In this way he became one of the new breed of Englishmen who lead the pleasant life of enjoying all the advantages of a country place without the trouble of running it, and the surer income that comes from business.

They are not wealthy but they are more than comfortably off. And recently—quite apart from the engagement of their son to a Royal princess—their fortunes took a decided turn for the better. Under the chairmanship of Peter Phillips, a company owning a large granite quarry sold out for £2·1-million. Mark's father said, 'My family had an interest in the company,' but modestly he would not say how much.

Peter and Anne Phillips are hunting people, as is their daughter Sarah, five years younger than Mark. They live and mix in a society which revolves around the meet. Mark's aunt, Miss Flavia Phillips, lives next door and is a horse trainer as well as being the joint owner with Mark of Great Ovation, the Olympic gold medal horse.

Peter Phillips has no blood link with Britain's aristocracy. On Mark's mother's side, the rich banking family of Tiarks are cousins.

Anne Phillips is a fair-haired, blue-eyed woman with a look of good breeding and the stance and seat of a horsewoman. She is the daughter of Brigadier John Tiarks who was an aide-de-camp to King George the

Sixth and she served in both the A.T.S. and the W.R.N.S. during World War II.

She runs her six-bedroomed house efficiently with the minimum of help and with the cheerful philosophy that what is not done today can be finished tomorrow. It is a cheerful, lived-in home with hunting prints on the walls, trophies of the chase on overmantels and tables, and copies of *Horse and Hounds* and *The Field* on the coffee tables.

*In the grounds of
Buckingham Palace, 1973*

Anne Phillips does most of her own cooking and, having discovered the greater ease of a house not big enough to have servants living in, enjoys the freedom from the regime imposed on her when she had staff.

So it was to a large extent among Mark's friends and not in Royal circles that the romance blossomed. Although a keen horsewoman Princess Anne had never taken to the hunting field before Mark Phillips came into her life. Yet she flouted public opinion to ride to hounds beside him.

Right through the hunting season the Princess was out, frequently borrowing a horse from her host. Usually her visit was kept a secret from the rest of the followers. She and Mark would join the hunt after it had moved off.

But there was one occasion with the Cheshire hunt when her splendid horsemanship was enough to reveal her identity. A rider fell by a fence. Princess Anne called 'Leave the horse to me,' and, clearing a three-foot fence on Moses, the bay gelding she had been lent, she caught up with the runaway, took her reins in one hand swinging low from the saddle, caught the horse cowboy-style and quietened it.

The collaborator in the horse-float episodes was Mrs Julian Sturgis. She agreed to let Mark smuggle the Princess on to the Sturgis' four-hundred-acre estate, Dauntsey Park, in a horse float.

'We have always heard that the Queen and Prince Philip approved right from the beginning,' Mrs Sturgis was happy to disclose once concealment was no longer necessary.

'Anne always came here with their full approval. Anne and Mark came down here and nobody realised it. They used to arrive in the horse-box together. They both have a great sense of humour.'

But lest anybody think these escapades were known only to the Queen and Patience Sturgis, Mrs Sturgis added: 'Even when they came to the park to relax, Anne's private detective was never far away."

Someone else who had a hand in fostering the romance but who maintained the utmost discretion was Mark Phillips' commanding officer.

Lieutenant-Colonel Maurice Johnston invited Princess Anne to his home, Haig House, at Catterick, Yorkshire. It was here that Lieutenant Mark Phillips introduced her to the blood sports that were to cause such a furore. Haig House, which is a conventional army-type house, strictly functional and quite devoid of glamour, was another place where Anne was able to get to know Mark better without too much pressure of publicity.

There were quiet weekends but also weekends when together they attended a hunt ball, a regimental dance, Then there was some more fox-hunting.

Mark Phillips now looks back on these weekends at Colonel Johnston's as some of the happiest and most significant in his courtship. 'We became friends and the friendship just grew', he says. 'We grew to love each other.'

The courtship of Anne and Mark

So Colonel Johnston was among the first to offer his congratulations and best wishes when the engagement was officially announced. But then he had been among the very first to know. In the way of army life it was no more than his duty. For a commanding officer has to keep a strict watch on his young subalterns. And even before Mark could approach the Royal family about his intentions, he had to have the permission of his commanding officer to arrange a marriage, even with a princess.

A baby

London in August is hot and humid and August, 1950, was no exception. Anyone who could get out of the city did, though there was more to it than escaping from the heat. Socially, it was pretty well imperative. For life, even in 1950, after the immense upheaval of World War II and despite the years of austerity which by then seemed to be stretching indefinitely ahead of the British, was determinedly following its traditional social pattern. For some people it was perhaps just a blind, stupid wish to believe that nothing had really changed; for others, it was simply an understandable, human desire to cling to things that were familiar.

The London social season was a formidable institution and few defied its rules. Even until World War II anyone in the social swim who had not managed to get

43

out of London in August pulled down the blinds and hid behind them in a kind of shame. Stories were still in circulation of poor creatures who covered their social disgrace by getting a trusted friend to send a postcard in their name from any fashionable, distant resort, saying they were 'having a wonderful time'.

In this year of 1950 society had managed through the summer to organise something like a season. There had been Royal Ascot, King George VI, recovering from his first serious illness, and Queen Elizabeth had held court at Buckingham Palace with presentations of debutantes and with garden parties where top hats and morning dress for men were still obligatory for those not still in uniform. All this, in spite of food rationing, clothes on coupons so that women looked like 'forces' sweethearts' for lack of new dresses, queues for cigarettes, rising taxation to pay for a new health service and a welfare state, and the realisation that, with India gone and Pakistan created, it was the swansong of the British Empire.

And in this particular August, society was now off to the moors, the highlands, their country estates. They were huntin', shootin' and fishin' all over the British Isles.

On the morning of 15 August it rained. By noon the lunchtime crowds were out and about in raincoats and umbrellas.

Suddenly the oppressive calm was broken. There was the boom, boom, boom of cannon from Hyde Park, church bells pealed and gradually flags began to unfurl and hang limply, waiting for a breeze to set them off in fluttering tribute.

This time few Londoners, who are usually so alert to events in their great city, knew—or cared—what all the banging and clanging was about. Not until a car drove down the Mall from Buckingham Palace, flying the Royal Standard, did it dawn on those who happened to be in the area that it might be a second baby to Princess Elizabeth, heiress presumptive to the throne, and her husband, Prince Philip.

Queen Elizabeth, the Queen Mother, in the natural, appealing way she has always had of slipping in a bit of news before an official announcement, leant out of the window of the car and said to the few passers by: 'It's a girl.'

So there had been some notable members of London Society in town in unfashionable August. Not only did the Royal mother decide to stay on in London to have her second baby in her own home, Clarence House, but her mother stayed in London, too, to be near her daughter. The Queen remained at Buckingham Palace although King George VI had gone on up to Balmoral to begin a much needed rest after rallying from his illness and to help him to face a heavy official programme.

Queen Elizabeth the Second is the least rebellious of women. In fact, her whole life is dedicated to maintaining the monarchial tradition. But this does not mean that she does not firmly, and quite frequently, reject rules which seem to her to fly in the face of common sense and convenience. And the birth of Princess Anne was one of these times.

A baby

Princess Anne in her own lifestyle follows this pattern. While her horsemanship has in the last few years revived such an interest in this sport that pony club membership has gone from two hundred-and-fifty to four hundred-and-two, she in no way conforms to the old rules of the horsey set. Princess Anne and her father Prince Philip are more often than not out sailing on the Glorious Twelfth, the traditional start of the grouse-shooting season. And with the use of planes of the Queen's flight, helicopter, or her own fast car on motorways running the length and breadth of the country, she is in and out of London in August, or any time that suits.

Without putting too fine a point to it, Princess Anne, born in 1950, had it made.

She may have arrived without the fuss and tension which came before the birth of her brother, Prince Charles, the heir to the throne, but she came more clearly into a new world. When the new baby's head was wet the thirty people who drank champagne at Clarence House were nearly all naval personnel from HMS *Magpie*, her father's new command.

Princess Anne was described as a 'lovely baby'. There was not a sour note anywhere. Newspapers pointed out that although her parents had an income of £50,000 a year 'there will be few new clothes for the princess', making those in Britain still struggling along on food and clothing coupons feel a bit better. It was pointed out, too, that 'as this is their second child the couple will now be entitled to the 5s. family allowance'.

47

Left, *At Frogmore, Windsor, with Prince Edward and the Queen, 1969*
Right, *At Badminton Horse Trials, 1973*
ver Left, *Oslo, Norway, 1971*
ver Right, *Dolphinarium, Blair Drummond, 1972*

London papers still had only a few pages to each issue, but once news editors got the idea that here was a good story, they devoted a considerable part of their restricted space to what was after all the fairly restricted life of a new-born baby. Wrote noted columnist Cassandra: 'Fortunately Anne can't read. But if she could I am sure Princess Anne Elizabeth Louise would let out a yell of laughter in derision or pure rage at the words of excruciating goo that have been written about her in the past forty-eight hours.'

Over the years when Princess Anne could read she undoubtedly let out many a yell of laughter at what was written about her.

On October 21, 1950, Anne was christened at Buckingham Palace, wearing the christening robes that date back to her great-great-great-grandmother Queen Victoria.

Her name, Anne, found favour in an unexpected way. It was a revival of the Stuarts' christian names, as Charles' had been.

At this time the feeling of restlessness in the British Commonwealth was growing more marked. Everywhere colonies were wanting to follow India and seek their independence; whether they were ready for it or not. The romantic flavour of the Stuarts was an added ingredient to the traditional view of the Throne as a stabilising influence in the Commonwealth.

Princess Anne's first public appearance was at a cocktail party for Commonwealth Prime Ministers after their annual conference in London five years later. The party was at Buckingham Palace and, wearing a pink party dress, the blonde princess curtsied prettily as Prince Philip introduced her around.

This impeccable behaviour owed much to the discipline of her nanny. Nanny Lightbody had been with the Duke and Duchess of Gloucester as nanny to Prince William, who was to be killed piloting his own plane in 1972, and his younger brother Prince Richard.

They had called her 'No Nonsense' Lightbody. And she stood for no nonsense from Anne either, who had plenty of character and could throw a tantrum as well as anybody.

Ulrica Forbes, the first artist to draw Princess Anne, then a child of just over three, recalls how strict Nanny Lightbody was. Anne had a heavy cold on the day of one sitting and wanted a sweet biscuit with her morning hot milk. But the rule was that the plain one must be eaten first, and rules were rules. 'I hid the plain biscuit beneath a cushion,' Ulrica Forbes confessed later, 'so that the poor little mite could have one break.'

Princess Anne's early childhood was overshadowed by the strain of King George VI's health. She was only a year old when it deteriorated so suddenly that doctors were called to Balmoral, where the Royal family were once again on holiday.

Princess Elizabeth and Prince Philip were preparing to set off for Canada on a five-week, coast-to-coast tour, but this had to be postponed for one week in early October until an operation for lung cancer was success-

fully performed on the King at Buckingham Palace.
Bearing this strain—and also, incidentally, the Royal
Seal, which as heiress presumptive she took with her in
case she became Queen while she was in Canada—
Princess Elizabeth went off with her husband, leaving
the two small children in the charge of Nanny Lightbody.

Gradually King George recovered, but there were
other changes for the Princess to face when she re-
turned. The Labour Government was out and the Con-
servatives in. The King named Winston Churchill as
his new Prime Minister.

A baby

There was an air of greater change about. The Festival of Britain was planned to inject new ideas into the arts and to increase their importance in the life of the average Briton. There was to be a new architecture, new industrial design. Plans for eight new towns to relieve congestion on London were under way. The city in which Anne was born was to have high-rise buildings instead of slums, space instead of overcrowding, air conditioning instead of stuffiness.

Princess Anne was only eighteen months old when, in February, 1952, King George VI died and her mother became Queen Elizabeth II. Princess Elizabeth and Prince Philip were in Kenya on the start of a Royal tour of Ceylon, Australia and New Zealand when the news came.

In later years Princess Anne was to visit the hotel where her mother had been spending a night-long vigil in a tree-house to watch wild animals when she became Queen.

Beside the lake in the grounds of Buckingham Palace, 1973

Sadly for Princess Anne she remembers nothing of her quite exceptional, hard-working and much loved grandfather. He had come to the throne quite unexpectedly after the abdication of his brother, the Duke of Windsor. If the abdication looked like rocking the monarchy, King George VI and his consort, Queen Elizabeth steadied it.

He was very much a family man. It was in a happy family environment that the new Queen grew up. And when she and Prince Philip with their two children, Charles and Anne, moved to Buckingham Palace they created a secure family atmosphere even in that unlikely setting.

Childhood

If there is one thing which marks the Queen of England off from much of England's upper classes, it is the amount of time she spent with her children when they were small and spends with them now. The image of the upper-class English child, passed across to a nanny, visited once a day in the nursery for a short time, then bundled off to boarding-school as soon as possible, is not just a figure of fiction; it is often grim reality.

Queen Elizabeth was a working woman, as more and more of her subjects were becoming. She was in her office on the dot of nine o'clock and her programme went on relentlessly. She was and is efficiency itself, running her life to a strict schedule. Her staff and servants would say: 'You could set your watch by her.' And she managed all this without much recourse to

53

Prince Philip's new gadgetry which was beginning to make the Palace look like an office efficiency exhibition.

But a good deal of her organising capacity went into planning her life so as to make as much time as she could for her children. Her other concern with them was to protect them from over-exposure at an early age.

This was easier. The grounds of Buckingham Palace are a sweeping eleven acres of lawns, gardens, lakes and trees. It is an idyllic setting for garden parties and receptions but it served equally for letting the children have their pets and plenty of room to roam wild. Here they could be secure from the crowds who had followed their prams when they were taken from Clarence House, which had very little in the way of grounds, for walks in St. James's Park.

Whenever it was possible, Queen Elizabeth changed her programme to fit in more time with the children. Prime Ministers were asked to come one hour later than the traditional time for their weekly visit to the Queen: she wanted to see her children at bathtime and read them a story before tucking them up in bed. As other mothers could.

If the Queen had no engagements she would have

Ethiopia, 1973

ellowknife, Canada,
ly 1970

lunch in the nursery with the children. Whenever possible she exercised the dogs in the Palace grounds with Princess Anne.

An astonished Archbishop was once brought into the family circle to find the Queen and her children in a semi-dark room 'hissing and booing the villain in front of a television set'.

Members of the Cabinet, diplomats, and representatives of Commonwealth countries soon became used to the line up of kiddycarts and tricycles in the spacious halls of the Palace as they walked along the red carpet to meet the Queen.

There was never a moment off-duty when the Queen did not have one or other of the children with her.

Princess Anne must surely have developed some of her interest in clothes from the innumerable fittings she has watched her mother have at the Palace. A Royal milliner once said to me that it was difficult to concentrate on the job because Princess Anne was pulling the hats out of their boxes and trying them on herself to gales of laughter from Charles.

At Balmoral the Queen gave Princess Anne and Prince Charles such a run of the place that the housekeeper, who had been with the Royal family all her life, complained to Prince Philip: 'The bairns are wearing out the carpets with their tricycles, running around the corridors'.

'Nonsense, they were worn out before we came here,' he retorted.

56

The Queen, more mildly, pointed out that, in fact, they were the original tartan carpets laid down by Queen Victoria.

As Princess Anne grew a little older, things began to relax a little on the nursery front. Miss Mabel Anderson, of Edinburgh, who had been assistant to Mrs Lightbody, replaced her and a much less rigid regime made for happier days for little Princess Anne.

Miss Catharine Peebles came as governess to Charles and Anne in the nursery where once the Queen and her sister had taken their lessons from Miss Marion Crawford, the noted 'Crawfie' whose books on her Royal charges disclosed so much of what went on behind the scenes that the expression, 'doing a Crawfie' every time a Royal confidence is broken, was born. It is said that when the first book was published Princess Elizabeth cried for three days on realising that her dear governess could not be trusted to keep to herself the private moments in the life of a growing girl.

The Queen was crowned in Westminster Abbey on June 2, 1953, and after her coronation was to embark with Prince Philip on a long Commonwealth tour. They were away for nearly six months visiting Bermuda, Jamaica, sailing through the Panama Canal and down the Pacific to Fiji. After that there was a two months' visit to New Zealand, then another two months in Australia. On the return journey the Queen visited Ceylon, the Cocos, Aden, Uganda, Tobruk, Malta and Gibraltar. It was all part of the Royal tradition of 'showing the crown', although subsequent events have

*Polo at Windsor,
June 1962*

shown that in spite of Elizabeth's tremendous personal effort, results were decidedly mixed.

Princess Anne was too young to remember much of these early comings and goings.

But the Queen remembers how at times she was resentful, and then there might be the tears and tantrums of a child, bewildered and frustrated at not quite knowing what it was all about. While she was away the Queen and Prince Philip would send back cards to the children. Occasionally they telephoned and spoke to Prince Charles. Anne would be lifted up to the phone to

58

hear their voices.

Presents for the children were showered on the Royal couple from every place they visited. But few of these were allowed into the nursery. Some went to hospitals, others, such as a Maori tiki, to a museum. A sailing boat, a present from Auckland, New Zealand, for Prince Charles, went up to Loch Muick where, in later years, he and Anne sailed her.

There was one souvenir of the long tour which the Queen gave Anne. It was her own bed from the ship *Gothic*, commissioned as a Royal yacht for the tour. Anne had it in her nursery and took it with her when she grew up and moved into her own suite of rooms in the Palace.

Anne was not quite four years old when she and Charles sailed in the newly commissioned Royal yacht *Britannia* to Tobruk to meet the Queen and Prince

Left, *1963 Windsor Horse Show*

Right, *Bridesmaid at the wedding of the Duke and Duchess of Kent, 1962*

Philip on the last leg of their Commonwealth tour. The meeting was private and there isn't so much as a photograph to record this precious moment when the months of separation ended.

The Queen had flown to Tobruk with Prince Philip. After laying wreaths on the graves of soldiers who had died there in World War II, she went on to visit King Idris of Libya and boarded her new yacht that was lying in the harbour.

The family then sailed to Malta, which has a very special place in their affections. When Elizabeth and Philip were married, he was serving in the Mediterranean fleet. Princess Elizabeth would fly to Malta to join her husband there from time to time. The announcement that the Princess was expecting her second child was made from Malta.

That baby was now a blue-eyed, golden-haired child who looked as if butter wouldn't melt in her mouth as she came down the gangway of *Britannia* in Valetta harbour. She looked as pretty as a picture as she stepped forward to get into the maroon Rolls Royce waiting for the Royal family. She may have thought so too, because the waiting crowd saw her catch a glimpse of herself in its glossy finish. She paused, looked again, preening herself slightly, got into the car.

On the parade ground in Malta she was the first to spot the little dog that inevitably runs on and steals the scene. At home when their pony was competing at Windsor it was Anne who saw him first and yelled, 'There's William, there's William,' slithering off her chair and knocking the Queen's programme to the ground.

It was not surprising, then, that the idea began to grow that although Prince Charles was a pleasant child with good manners, he was rather dull compared with his sister.

The Queen, with an understanding of children, laughed and said, 'Little girls appear so much brighter at that age. Particularly if they have an elder brother.'

Such doubts have long been dispelled. Charles may not even now always show the liveliness of his sister, but he is undoubtedly witty—perhaps the only real wit in the Royal family—and highly intelligent.

The Queen and Prince Philip did not have very advanced ideas on bringing up children but they had a lot of common sense. Before the long tour it had been suggested that the Queen Mother could move into the Palace to look after the children in their parents' absence. 'I can bring up my children myself, thank you,' was the Queen's unexpectedly sharp response to her advisers.

Princess Anne was five years old when she began lessons in the Palace nursery. She may not have liked them much, but it was obvious that she was happy to be occupied and to feel that at last she was catching up with her elder brother.

Their governess, Miss Peebles, wove lessons around life as the children knew it, bringing in the names of the kind of people who came and went from the Palace. Thus their education became in some ways a much truer picture of life around them than it is for many children.

The children called her 'Misspy' and she had come, in that way the Royal family have of passing those they can trust from one member to the next, from the household of the late Princess Marina.

The schoolroom at Buckingham Palace is next to the high-ceilinged day and night nurseries. These rooms had been used by the Queen and Princess Margaret. When the two princesses grew up, the suite was redecorated and refurnished as Princess Margaret's private quarters. It was here that what was known as the Clan Margaret in the late 'forties would gather before an evening out. It was here that the long-playing records she collected—as good as any collection of the time—were stored in a cabinet given by Queen Mary.

When the Queen moved into Buckingham Palace the rooms became once more a nursery suite, much as they had been in her day. The comfortable settee and deep armchairs were re-covered with the Royal family's favourite chintz to match the curtains, the records went to Clarence House with Margaret and the cupboard was once more filled with toys.

There was one notable change: a television set. Princess Anne, in the years ahead, was to sprawl full length on the floor, her face propped in her hands, watching westerns with rare delight. As a girl of her times the background to her study and reading was always pop music from a transistor radio.

Anne was adventurous and was first up the trees and

on the the roof at Windsor Castle. She was also a good sparring partner. When Prince Philip bought the children boxing gloves he had to take them away again, 'until they learn something of Queensberry rules', he said. 'They nearly knocked each other out.'

When Prince Charles went off to his pre-prep school, Hill House in Knightsbridge, his first front tooth was missing. Dropped out, or knocked out?

Anne, who so far hadn't found other little girls the most exciting company, found herself sharing lessons with two, Caroline Hamilton and Susan Babington-

Left, *Princess Anne with King Olaf and Crown Princess Sonja of Norway, June 1971*

Right, *Mule riding in the Simian Mountains, Ethiopia, 1973*

Smith, who came daily to the Palace. Soon the three were getting on well together. Caroline and Susan were the same age as Anne and by a combined effort could stand up to her assertiveness. Besides, lessons with Anne were never dull.

When the Queen found in the summer of 1959 that she was to have another baby she and Prince Philip were overjoyed. The Queen thought perhaps that the new baby might go somewhere towards solving some of the problems that were beginning to weigh on her.

If the baby were a boy it would strengthen the male line of succession to the throne. And the Queen had told a close friend that she wanted to protect Anne from being a girl second in succession. 'I don't want her to have the life of my sister Margaret.'

If Anne had remained second in line she would not have been free to live as easily and informally as she has been able to. And there would also have been much more involved in any marriage she might have made. Mark Phillips, nice and suitable as he looks as husband to a Royal princess in Britain in 1973, might not have seemed quite suitable to a Princess who could be called upon at any time to succeed her elder brother if chance befell.

A few hours before the third baby was born at Buckingham Palace on February 19, 1960, Prince Philip said, 'I do so hope it's a boy.' Prince Andrew disappointed nobody.

While everyone rejoiced in the Queen's happiness she whispered to her husband: 'How tiny! I'd forgotten that the other two were ever so small.'

Childhood

There was nine and a half years' difference between Anne and the baby who was to change the whole course of her life.

Throughout the ornamental, gilded rooms of Buckingham Palace there was the same special atmosphere that there is in any home where there is a new baby.

Anne was in her element. She skipped lessons more than once to race down the Palace stairs for yet another peep at her baby brother. Prince Charles, given a half-day from Cheam school to see the new baby, stayed home for the weekend.

A Royal photographer, Antony Armstrong-Jones, hung about quite a lot, ostensibly teaching Prince Philip how to take pictures of his new son. Princess Margaret was back and forth to the Palace, in and out of the Queen's bedroom.

*Lake Abyata,
Ethiopia, 1973*

Princess Margaret had promised that she would wait until the baby arrived before formally asking for permission to marry.

The young prince was a week old when Queen Elizabeth, the Queen Mother announced the betrothal of her daughter, the Princess Margaret, to Mr Antony Armstrong-Jones.

Anne as a schoolgirl

Princess Anne had much the same schooling as her future husband, Mark Phillips. She went to Benenden, an upper-middle-class school for girls, while he was at Marlborough, an upper-middle-class school for boys.

The difference was that she was a Royal princess, the only daughter of a British reigning monarch to go to boarding school. Although they tried to make her just one of the girls it was not easy. Having your mother, the Queen, arrive for speech days did cast a different aura over the occasion. Having your detective on the alert at the school at all times certainly marked you out from your fellows. And it was difficult not to fall into a clique of girls who had connections with the Palace.

Anne went to Benenden when she was 13. It is an independent school for girls in Kent, where Princesses from other countries are sent for a good, all-round English education.

A Benenden girl has just the right accent, not too 'posh', not too 'debbie', but distinctive. Benenden girls are trained to take a place in the world. They have a high entry at universities and an even higher infiltration into the world of commerce. As secretaries in the United States they can command a high salary; not only for the efficiency expected of them but for that little extra something bred into them at Benenden.

Benenden takes pride in the fact that its girls never lose touch. All old girls are still called 'seniors', because,

Jamaica, August 1966

as they say, 'once a Benenden, always a Benenden'.

How does Anne measure up? Since the Princess left school, her Royal duties have meant that she has had little spare time for such things as the annual reunion. Gradually she seems to have lost touch, and her circle of schoolfriends has dwindled to one whom she looked up while she was on a lengthy Royal tour and to one or two others she meets occasionally at the milliner's or at equestrian events.

But while Princess Anne was at Benenden she was very much a part of the school. She slipped easily into the life of a schoolgirl among some three hundred others.

The Queen's decision to send Anne there was a difficult one. She enjoyed the company of her daughter. Princess Anne was a natural, fun-loving girl who brought to the Palace the kind of life it needs. It is a lonely place, in spite of the great number of people coming and going. Princess Anne herself once described it: 'Big rooms, draughty corridors where my young brothers play football. I doubt if anyone would like it for long.'

Anne, too, was the apple of her father's eye. She would be much missed by him. What father can resist the flattery of a little daughter who grows up to take after him? And who would help him groom his polo ponies every season?

But the Queen made up her mind to send Anne away to school because she sensed a growing restlessness in her. Charles was now at Gordonstoun, and Anne wanted companionship of her own age. The two girls still came for lessons each day but went home at four o'clock. And there was the weekly meeting of the First Buckingham Palace Girl Guides in the summerhouse of the Palace grounds on fine days and inside, in the big room used as a cinema, when it was wet. As well, there was a new baby, Prince Andrew, in the nursery.

But Princess Anne was growing up. The Queen had begun to share the concern of her friends who were also mothers of teenage girls.

'What can you do with them!' the Queen cried one day in mock horror, throwing up her hands as the door opened on Anne's room.

And Anne's room was much like that of any girl of her generation: on the walls a gallery of colour pictures from the glossy magazines of her pop idols—and the door firmly closed to intruders. 'There'll be a "Private" notice on it before long,' the Queen's closest friend, who had been through it all, warned.

Anne could, in common with most girls her age, be moody. And she was strong willed. She needed companions who could stand up to her. Anne had qualities of leadership, as she had proved in the Guides, who had themselves voted her into positions of authority. But it was time for her to test herself in a wider field.

Prince Philip certainly thought so. In later years the Queen said that even after Anne went to Benenden she wasn't sure it was the right thing. But after Anne's enthusiastic 'Yes' to the suggestion, there was no turning back.

Getting into a school like Benenden isn't easy. Not even for Anne could standards be lowered. If she was to keep up with the rest of her form she must improve her weak subjects; mathematics for instance.

It is typical of Anne's character that when she wants something badly, whether her first car for which she had to save, her first rosettes at the riding clubs, her first big events in the equestrian field, she will go all out for it.

Anne was no swot, but once she got her head down she was over the first hurdle. After that it was easy. And throughout her schooldays she was to find that although she was not scholarly, exams did not bother her overmuch.

When she left Benenden Princess Anne had six O-levels and, to the disappointment of her teachers who had expected better, two moderate A-levels. Just enough to go to university, had she been so minded. She was even qualified to enter for Oxford or Cambridge because she had passed the Use of English examination, an additional requirement.

But, 'I don't think I was ever academically good material,' she said some time after leaving school. 'I'm not much good at concentrating for long.'

When the Queen got the good news that Anne had qualified for Benenden she lost no time in making the announcement from Buckingham Palace. But not before Miss Elizabeth Clarke, the good-looking headmistress at Benenden, had told the school; she did not want them to be the last to know.

71

Benenden, proud of its reputation as one of the happiest schools in England, 'And not at all fashionable', the governors insisted, was now faced with a slight problem: would having Princess Anne at the school change things?

'I do hope it isn't going to spoil it for everyone,' said a senior, the wife of a governor. 'Our unpretentiousness has been the very heart of Benenden.'

They need not have worried.

There was a lot of publicity at first. But after the Queen's appeal to the news media to keep the coverage of Anne at school down to a minimum, the problem more or less disappeared.

Getting ready to go off to boarding-school had its exciting moments for Princess Anne as well as its sad ones.

She said good-bye to the Girl Guides. From now on there would be no more boisterous meetings, no panto-mimes at the Palace, no tea and buns with the Queen after an afternoon's guiding. The troop disbanded. They had come as a company from Westminster, a cross-section of the children living within a stone's throw of the Palace, the daughters of tradesmen, artisans, professional men, a taxi driver. They were children who called a spade a spade, or anything else they could lay tongue to. Later in life when it was suggested that Princess Anne had picked up her salty language from her father, one of the Guides retorted proudly, 'Nonsense. She got it from us.'

Anne as a schoolgirl

Anne, getting ready for school, was happy, bustling. It confirmed Prince Philip's long-felt suspicions that she had felt out of things. Subconsciously? Perhaps.

The Queen, however, did not feel then or at any time in her life that she made any difference between her children. Although Anne was at times hard to manage she was always straightforward. If she had had any hard feelings, or thought she was being neglected, she would have blurted something out.

Before the annual holiday at Balmoral, all seventeen pieces of Princess Anne's uniform were delivered and alterations made. Anne, at thirteen was a good stock size but taller than most girls of her age. So hems were dropped.

The Queen interrupted her holiday to bring Anne to Benenden at the start of term in September, 1963. It was the Queen's first appearance in public since the announcement a few days before that she was expecting her fourth child early in the New Year.

When they arrived at the school, a grey stone mansion once the home of the Earl of Cranbrook, all the girls were lined up outside to greet them. Not, one would have thought, the best way to introduce a new girl whose Royal parents hoped would be treated 'just like any other girl'.

Left, *Badminton, 1971*

Centre, *New Zealand, 1970*

Right, *1973 Amberley Horse Trials*

Benenden's uniform is a navy tunic, white shirt, white knee-length socks, a choice of pastel dresses for summer and a dramatic, ankle-length cloak, in navy-blue lined with the colours of your house, for outdoors. Anne's was orange for Guledford.

The Queen, looking down on the ranks of girls, exclaimed: 'Oh, they all look alike!'

Wasn't that supposed to be the idea? No distinction, whether your family were stockbrokers, professionals, in trade or royal. The uniform was designed for this. Yet it gave Anne a new distinction. She looked less of a tomboy, more of a nice English miss.

The girls at Benenden had been asked to forget that she was Royal, to call her Anne. And there were to be no curtsies. For their part, the girls wanted to know what she would contribute to the school.

Benenden's physical training mistress, Miss Crittenden, had been an international lacrosse player and was delighted when Anne chose to play in one of the school teams. She was tall, had her father's quick eye for the ball and went on to play with her section at the School's Lacrosse Tournament in 1968.

She did rather less well in tennis although Prince Philip had brought Dan Maskell to the Palace to coach her. 'I can't sustain my game when the sets get too serious,' she said. So she took to swimming in the unheated pool instead.

Princess Anne did not take judo lessons at Benenden although it was rumoured that she would. Margot

Satheye, a leading expert who had a two-hour weekly class at the school, was disappointed but said the Princess was a fan.

The Princess did, however, try rock-climbing. These expeditions must have caused the Queen some apprehension. On a visit to a grammar school she remarked, 'I sometimes wonder if rock climbing isn't more dangerous than is made out.'

But Miss Cynthia Gee, the Princess' house-mistress, who went with the girls on these expeditions, stoutly maintained that 'climbing was made out to be more dangerous than it is'.

It would be easy to think that life was all sport because the few photographs of her during these years were mostly taken on holidays at sporting events.

But Anne tried her hand at many things. She had a shot at the oboe, a notably hard instrument, but dropped that. Piano lessons, which had started at the Palace, went on relentlessly. She took up pottery, jived at the dancing club, taught the others highland reels, sang in the school choir. Though she was never in the same class as Prince Charles as an actor, she was in the Drama Club and could clown or mimic or use a broad dialect. At the Christmas break-up party in Anne's last term she was a sailor, and the Queen had the joy of seeing her daughter reeling drunkenly around the stage in Purcell's *Dido and Aeneas*.

One thing Benenden could not eliminate entirely was her restlessness. Like Prince Philip she was always in a hurry. 'She would come rushing round corridors, which was forbidden, at such a pace you couldn't get an arm out quickly enough to stop her,' one of the mistresses complained.

Princess Anne paid a great deal of attention to her appearance while she was at school. She began to experiment with hair styles and to develop the variety of styles which she still wears at times.

At the Sunday evening informal suppers she took her turn on the roster for serving the cold food, washed up afterwards wearing a striped linen apron, wiped down

1971 Badminton Horse Trials

the tables, dried and polished the cutlery and re-arranged the dining-room. Nobody was more surprised than the Queen when she heard about this. Her daughter had never shown any signs of being domesticated.

Anne even learned to cook a hot meal. But did she like it? 'Well,' says Anne, 'it's fun at a barbecuc if you are more than cook's offsider.' And cook is her father.

But of all her activities the weekly riding lessons were the highlight. She was, of course, privileged in that her horse High Jinks was brought from the Royal stables to be installed at Moat House, a well known riding-school near Benenden.

Here Princess Anne had lessons from Mrs Hatton-Hall who, as Cherry Kendall, had been a well known competitive rider. Her instructor had started the riding school some years before and was a member of the senior judges' panel.

Had it not been for Mrs Hatton-Hall, Princess Anne might never have gone as far in competitive riding, and so might never have met Mark Phillips at equestrian events. For it was at Moat House that she got the grounding that was to take her to championship class.

The younger Princess Anne on a pony had been, like most youngsters, concerned only with jumping and going hell-for-leather across country. Now, while at Benenden, she was to learn at her riding-school that the basis of good equitation is dressage, to be applied and understood by both horse and rider.

Princess Anne's enthusiasm was aroused. Her ambition to be known for her own achievement and not for

77

her birth was sparked off. She worked desperately hard to be included in an equine quadrille championship at the Horse of the Year show in 1968, the year she finished school.

Working girl

An engineer? Because she is mechanically minded. A career in television? She's so quick witted and never seems at a loss for an answer. Something to do with children? She's so good with them and they take to her. One of the professions? But perhaps not, because she's not going to university.

What then? Once Princess Anne's schooldays were over she had every career wished on her by the press except the typing pool. When she spoke up for herself, she made it clear, if not in these words: 'I'll be what I am.'

Princess Anne Elizabeth Alice Louise stood fourth in line to the throne. As the only daughter of the Queen she had had her career laid down on the day she was born and all her training was to prepare her for it.

79

Being a princess was her job.

How she handled her job, however, was in large part up to her. She was certainly intelligent enough to say to herself, 'All right. It has its limitations but what job hasn't?'

If she had been less conscientious, less her mother's daugher, she could have taken up her Royal duties lightly, skimming over the surface, just getting through the minimum and perhaps with marriage dipping out altogether, leaving it to her parents and brothers to soldier on.

She could have given herself far more time with her horses, put in more training for championships and eventing, as many of the British Horse Society hoped she would.

Keeping her name out of the Court circular would have kept it in big type on the Sports Pages. But Princess Anne made riding her hobby not her whole life and fitted in training whenever she could. She got up early in the morning to drive to the stables, and would go straight from a foreign tour to a work-out with her horses. She would give up her holidays to fly down from Balmoral for extra riding lessons, more training.

But all this time her official programme was expanding. More and more visits were crowded in at home, longer and further travels abroad. She began to emerge as a highly individual, good-looking rather than pretty girl with a mind of her own.

She was a hard person for people to make up their minds about. Sometimes charming and smiling on the

Top Left, *With Jomo Kenyatta, President's Pal*
Nairobi, Kenya, I
Top Right, *On Safari in Kenya, I*
Lower Left, *Maoris in New Zealand, I*
Lower Right, *Khartoum, Sudan, I*

job, sometimes moody and detached. Sometimes a notably well dressed girl in the fashion swim, sometimes a girl who cared more for the casual.

She was a horsey girl, in the championship class, and that was to make her front-page news. But she was also a cover girl all over continental Europe with her wide smile and beautiful teeth. Her blue eyes that could register all shades of mood and emotion looked out at you from bookstalls all over Europe. European magazines, notably the French, never ceased to record the slightest bit of tittle tattle, or to fabricate their own news. Even the Japanese *Asahi Shimbun* reported that 'Princess Anne is the "new star" of the Royal family' and opined that 'What is more, her liberal demeanour, overstepping the bounds of the past practices of the Royal family, will no doubt be one of the reasons why the public feels closer to the Princess.'

'Overstepping the bounds of the past practices of the Royal family', Princess Anne got her career off to a flying start in 1969 by handling her own public relations, something unthinkable in the Queen or Princess Margaret's day.

Anne had a cocktail party at Buckingham Palace for the Press early in the year. The guests were all young and that night the idea that you don't speak to Royalty until they have spoken to you flew out the window.

The Princess, sipping a glass of coke she managed to make last the whole evening, circulated. Every guest was presented. After that the conversational ball spun back and forth, most often landing in the Princess's court. As the drinks flowed, so the guests became less inhibited and polite party chat became pretty rapid-fire questioning.

Most of the time the Princess was forthcoming, but she turned some questions aside with great diplomacy. She talked about herself. 'I've nothing particular to look forward to,' she remarked in a burst of frankness.

She was decidedly wrong! She has done very well at her job, has excelled at her chosen sport and now is head over heels in love with Mark Phillips and he with her. They are both champion riders in fierce competition with each other, which gives their lives an added zest.

But the first party for the Press was such a success that, shortly after, the Princess gave another. In the years that followed Princess Anne was to receive many journalists at the Palace, particularly before some very special occasion, such as a long tour.

Invitations to her Press receptions are typed on Buckingham Palace notepaper; acceptances are by telephone. But although they are cocktail parties, guests must arrive on time, and before the Princess enters the room. Everyone is presented but after that there are no more formalities.

These informal parties have undoubtedly taught Princess Anne a lot about handling people. They have developed her skill in fending awkward questions, as one senior newspaperman learnt when he asked her, on the eve of the Royal family's visit to Australia for the 1970 Captain Cook bicentenary, how much she knew about republican feeling in Australia. The Princess fell back on feminine wile. Like a small girl who doesn't quite understand the question, she replied: 'All I know about Australia is the map we had to draw at school, the bays, the capes, the inlets.' Then she added in the rather abrupt way she has of finishing off a conversation she doesn't much care for: 'When I've been there I'll be able to tell you more.'

These were happy days for Princess Anne and the

Princess Anne with two Princesses in Tonga, March 1970

Aboard the Russian ship Skritinii, *Massawa, Ethiopia, 1973*

press, and it might have gone on so forever, if horse-riding hadn't come into it.

She was a photographer's delight. Her figure had fined down; her clothes were trendy; her hairstyles were always new and interesting; and she had managed to get around the old Royal rule that women shouldn't wear hats that covered their faces. She wore hats with wide, dashing brims.

One of the top London photographers declared she had a 'face that changes every day'. But he felt her smile was worth waiting for.

When Princess Anne gave a photographic session to a sophisticated fashion photographer, more used to top models than a princess, he said afterwards, 'I had great trouble in not calling her darling.'

1969, the year she began her public life, was the beginning of that short, silly phase, 'Swinging London'. The

85

Beatles were still around, the Stones still big, the Shrimp was still a name, there was Twiggy, and now, of all things, the British had a swinging princess. Reporters were delighted with the copy she provided. She had them hopping joyously as she went off to discotheques, nightclubs, late suppers or danced on stage at the end of the musical, *Hair*. She even told them where she bought her undies.

It was not until she reached championship class as a horsewoman, and until no one would believe she was not in love with one or other of the Olympic candidates, that this relationship with the Press soured.

Then, on one occasion, when the cameramen closed right in on her, she called in a voice strident with rage, 'You get my goat. Can't you see you're frightening the horses? They don't understand.'

It didn't happen all the time; it didn't really happen often. But a girl of her drive and energy, her ambition to excel, and with a touch of Prince Philip's volatility could hardly also be a model of forbearance.

Yet she could be magnificently co-operative. At the Spanish Riding School in Vienna, when she was mounted on the white Lippizaner stallion Siglavia Bona she put him through his paces right up to the difficult piaffe. Then, to satisfy the 'Just one more picture, Your Royal Highness', she went through the performance again. All this time she was tired and flushed from the high temperature she was still running after a bout of influenza that had delayed her arrival to join the Queen and Prince Philip.

86

Princess Anne's rages are quickly spent. Every photographer knew what she meant when she presented the Photographer of the Year Award of 1970 and said she was always happy to be with them on the old principle, 'if you can't beat them, join them'.

Much of Princess Anne's public life is ceremonial, with flags, bunting, bands and curtsies. Repeated endlessly, they are considered important as a measure of the Crown's service to the nation and its interest in her people.

Princess Anne, in common with every member of the Royal family, takes a very great pride in her contribution to the smooth running of each occasion, the good feeling after a difficult job has gone off well. When she goes abroad on a State visit with the Queen and Prince Philip ceremonial is scarcely less rigid and opportunities for some little thing going wrong are often far greater.

The Princess has to do her homework well. And she has a trained eye to take in the scene so that there won't be any last-minute shuffling about or clumsy moves. She can sit perfectly still on a dais for long stretches of time without fidgeting with gloves, handbag or programme.

On many occasions Princess Anne is playing a secondary role to her mother, as when the Queen is receiving an address of welcome and making her reply, or there is a reception line and presentations, or they are watching some display or ceremonial. Then it is the Princess' Royal duty to make no move that could attract attention to herself. It would be wrong for her to wave and smile, no matter how many people try to catch her attention. And children frequently do.

This is a delicate situation that is not always understood. Because the Princess' face in repose can look bored, even sulky, she is often and sometimes quite unfairly credited with these moods.

When Princess Anne has her own programme she generally manages very well. Experience has taught her that while children quickly get over any feeling of shyness, officials and their wives can often remain tight-lipped and nervous right to the end of a Royal engagement; the only thing is to smile, chat and carry on.

Princess Anne is a girl who, given the first opportunity, airs her opinions, although these do not in general have a greater depth than those of the average twenty-three year old. To some students demonstrating for peace she said: 'How can you *demonstrate* for peace?'

She gave her views on women's liberation without being asked, simply taking the chance while launching a frigate, *Amazon*. In her speech she began by wondering why she had been chosen to launch the frigate and said: 'I reckon I found the answer in this piece of information pertaining to the Amazons, those formidable forerunners of the women's liberation movement with whom, incidentally, I have no sympathy. They were, apparently, at their most formidable on horseback.'

'She knows nothing about our struggle,' retorted a spokesman for Women's Liberation. 'A woman in her

Top, *Jumping with Doublet, 197*
Lower Left, *Arriving in Sydney, 197*
Lower Right, *Curtsey to a King, Grand Palace
Bangkok, Thailand, 197*

position of influence should be helping us instead of sabotaging our efforts.'

Before Princess Anne visited the United States in July, 1970, *Life* magazine gave its readers some advice on what to talk to her about. 'Don't,' it advised its readers, 'tire Princess Anne asking questions about women's hats, although she will be receptive to a chat about tanks and sub-machine guns.' This wasn't, of course, because Mark Phillips was an officer in a tank regiment and a girl in love had understandably picked up some knowledge of her loved one's job. This was three years ago when Mark Phillips to Anne was just another competitor in equestrian events.

It was because Princess Anne has herself driven a Chieftain tank and can fire from the hip with the best of them. She is Colonel-in-chief of the 14/20th King's Hussars and on her first visit to them in Paderborne, West Germany, she added a bit of excitement to the routine inspection by taking control of a fifty-ton tank. She is the only girl ever to have driven such a powerful tank. But adjusting her head-phones she was off and away over a muddy, hilly circuit for three miles, breaking the speed record for tanks—more than thirty miles an hour on the trip back.

Would she like to do it again? she was asked. 'Well,' she said with a laugh, 'I wish someone would give me one for Christmas.'

Soon afterwards she was out of overalls and into an army combat jacket, then firing a Sterling machine-gun at five hundred and seventy-five rounds a minute. Rat-atat-tat, the Princess fired from the shoulder—ten rounds with two bulls eyes. Then twenty rounds from the hip, scoring eleven hits.

Not everyone was pleased with these pictures of the Princess as a pistol-packing momma, but she has done it again on manoeuvres and there hasn't been a murmur.

Princess Anne has been a terrific personal success with the Army (quite apart from picking a soldier for her bridegroom). She dines with the officers of the King's Hussars in mess and drinks the toast with them to the Emperor. This is a very special one, one of those things which outsiders tend to think childish but which are part of service life. It involves the silver chamber-pot the Hussars captured from the King of Spain, Napoleon's brother.

It was clear than that Princess Anne had decided that her career, although prescribed for her, would be one of action. Action is what she likes. Other Royal ladies are not exactly unfamiliar with modern equipment, new inventions, weapons of war, fast cars and so on. A never-ending display is put on for them. But Princess Anne was the first not merely to look but to test.

At a visit to the Police Cadet Training School she climbed into the driving seat of a police car and took it on the skid pan. The car slipped and slithered but the Princess never lost control. Round and round she went, cheered on by a small crowd who hung over the ropes admiringly.

'I felt I was part of the car,' she said as with some

reluctance she handed over to the police. Their comment: 'That's the mark of an experienced driver.'

Anne was getting a good deal of excitement out of some of her public engagements, and she was also generating a good deal of her own. When she was scarcely out of her teens she was very much a public figure in her own right. Girls copied her wide-brimmed rakish hats (so much so that she was nicknamed the Duchess of Luton, Luton being the centre of the British women's hat-making industry).

As she drove through the gates of Paderborne, fingering the diamond crest of her regiment, the soldiers may have been proud that she had driven a Chieftain tank; but the band struck up, *Oh, You Beautiful Doll*. And beautiful, indeed, she looked.

A girl who can stand up for herself

Princess Anne was a young woman and there was a big, wide world waiting for her.

The Queen was so delighted to have her daughter with her and Prince Philip on the Captain Cook Bicentenary tour of Fiji, Tonga, New Zealand and Australia in 1970 that she mentioned it in her first speech. She talked of the pleasure she and her husband were taking in introducing their daughter to 'so many places we have been to before'.

The Royal party flew out from wintry London to join the Royal yacht *Britannia* at Lautoka in the Fiji islands for their cruise through the South Pacific. It was the longest air journey Princess Anne had ever made and it took her into a new and exotic world.

The tropical sun had just set over the green fields of

sugar cane, the glow still filtering through the cocoanut palms and bathing the island in reddish-golden light when they stepped from the aircraft at Nadi international airport. Princess Anne was wearing a yellow mini dress and a white-flowered hat. Dusk follows sunset rapidly in the tropics so the Rolls Royce taking the Queen, her husband and Princess Anne along the fifteen miles of coastline to Lautoka was floodlit inside. This meant that the first view the Fijians had of Anne was as a golden princess sitting on the fold-down seat of the car in front of her parents.

They passed through villages lit by flaming torches, some carried by Fijians in grass skirts who ran beside the Royal car. A bonfire burst into flames toward the end of the journey, then a long roll of native drums told the villagers the visitors had arrived.

Wherever the Royal party went in Fiji there was a special welcome for Princess Anne. The Queen had been there twice before, but the Fijians were happy now to see her daughter.

The Royal yacht *Britannia* left Lautoka before midnight and sailed into Suva harbour the following morning. Six handsome Fijian chiefs went on board. They were glistening with cocoanut oil, wearing leaf skirts with tapa tops, garlanded with leis, and wore anklets and wristlets of shells and dried seed pods which rattled as they moved.

The chiefs presented the Queen with three whales' teeth, the traditional gesture of welcome, and invited the visitors ashore. A quarter of a million people—the largest crowd ever seen in the capital of the Fijian islands—were waiting to cheer them in streets hung with freshly picked hibiscus.

The loudest shouts came from children: 'Welcome, welcome, Princess Anne.'

Fiji was on the eve of independence. So Princess Anne was to see how the colony was emerging into nationhood, part of her education in political science. But she found Fiji the unspoiled place and its people the friendly people her parents had told her about.

In a morning of ceremonial welcome there was the traditional drinking of kava, the native brew. Princess Anne's cup was filled to the brim. Prince Philip leant forward and said grinning: 'They've given her a bucketful.'

The taste is slightly bitter. But a Fijian remarked that 'she drank it with the dignity of Queen Mary'.

One of the Royal visits was to the new university. It was then housed in a disused air-force hangar but in those sheds there were already some four hundred and fifty students working hard for their degrees. The Queen had granted the university a Royal charter and, although around one hundred universities had been established throughout the Commonwealth since the war, this was the first time she had presented the charter in person.

When the pro-chancellor of the University of the Pacific, Msiofo Fetaui Mata'afa, a tall, handsome woman, said eloquently: 'We have the courage, the gaiety and the joy of doing something worthwhile' the Princess joined in the sustained ovation.

95

The next visit was to a housing estate at Raiwanga. Princess Anne's interest was close and informed enough for her to begin making comparisons in size and rentals between some of the two-bedrooms in this estate with some of those in England.

Then the unexpected, of which Royalty is always wary, happened. A baby crawled across the floor of a flat Anne was inspecting and grabbed the shiny metal heel of the Princess's shoe. The heel had a tiny chain trim and the baby got its fingers into this. Immobilised for a moment or two, there was nothing for the Princess to do but to slip her shoe off and finally retrieve it from the child.

There was thunderous applause as the Princess left Raiwanga. Ear-splitting wolf whistles followed her from youths who suddenly appeared, like flocks of birds, on balconies, roofs and scaffolding.

The Queen and Prince Philip, waiting at the car for

Princess Anne with Emperor Haile Selassie during a Naval evening in Massawa, Ethiopia, 1973

their daughter, heard them and turning to each other exchanged smiles, proud parents with their daughter on her first big tour of the Commonwealth.

On the evening of that first day Princess Anne stood on the deck of *Britannia* as she slipped out of harbour. A massive Fijian choir sang the islands' farewell song, 'Isalei'. The wake of *Britannia*, as she moved out, was awash with flowers as women threw the garlands from around their necks into the water. It was an emotional yet satisfying good-bye, unlike anything the Princess had known before.

As darkness enfolded the scene the Princess remained on deck, watching Suva, which had given her such a touching welcome, recede and finally fade. Only the voices of the choir drifting over the water still came to her. As they, too, died away Anne gave one last wave, caught in the light of the rising full moon. Princess Anne remained on deck long after the others had gone below, enjoying the quietness and the solitude.

The next port of call was Tonga, which Captain Cook had called the Friendly Isles. In 1953 after Elizabeth's coronation in London, to which the Tongan Queen Salote drove in an open carriage through pouring rain to the joy of the London crowds, the English Queen had paid a visit to the island queen in her small kingdom. Now it was Salote's son King Taufa'Alau Tupou, a cocoanut mat encircling his enormous girth, who welcomed the Royal party to Tonga.

On a scenic tour of the island Princess Anne was to

97

see where Captain Cook had landed in 1777 and stocked up with fresh supplies. Cook recorded that the Tongans 'were more desirous to give than to receive'; and they were not short in generosity to the Royal visitors.

Soon in the broiling midday sun the two Royal families and hundreds of guests sat down to a feast even more sumptuous than that set before Queen Elizabeth twenty years before. Tourism and a touch of sophistication had come to Tonga, which now had its first international hotel, an airport and a weekly flying service. So there were *haute cuisine* touches to the dishes of freshly boiled lobster and fish straight from the sea.

Otherwise the meal was traditional, spread out on low tables on the Mali—a greensward and meeting place for the people beside the King's palace. As well as seafood, there were thirteen hundred succulent young sucking pigs which were spit-roasted, more than that number of plump chickens barbecued Tongan-style, and tropical fruits piled high in baskets.

Princess Anne sat with her hosts, just slightly raised above the ground on a dais. She tucked her legs beneath her, and, following the custom of the islanders, ate with her fingers.

Later, on the visit to the Royal burial ground, Princess Anne planted a tree alongside those of the Queen and Prince Philip in commemoration of Queen Salote.

When *Britannia* sailed the ship's decks may not have been piled high with food as Captain Cooks ship was but plenty of fresh fruit, sucking pig, chickens and lobsters went into the refrigerators.

Princess Anne has always loved *Britannia*. Some of her happiest holidays have begun with a cruise around the west coast of Britain in the Royal yacht on the way to Balmoral.

The yacht is very much a home away from home for the Royal family, particularly on long tours. To return to *Britannia* and find their own cabins, cosy and chintzy, with their books, television sets and transistor radios, just as they left them, their clothes in the ship's wardrobes, little personal things around, and their own beds to sleep in, is so much more relaxing than the endless run of overnight stays on shore. And life aboard ship offers blessed privacy.

On *Britannia* the Queen can return hospitality as effortlessly as though she were at Buckingham Palace or Windsor Castle. There is a non-stop round of parties whenever *Britannia* is berthed.

Princess Anne had been looking forward to the voyage in *Britannia*, sailing down the South Pacific to New Zealand. But the anticipation proved more exciting than the reality.

'Unfortunately I am not a good sailor,' she explained afterwards. 'And this was the longest trip I remember on *Britannia*.' She found the weather against her. 'It was too blustery to play deck tennis. The wind was even blowing the quoits overboard.

'And when we land no sooner do I get my land legs than we are off and I have to get my sea legs.'

When the Queen and Prince Philip had the quite

brilliant idea of changing the pattern of Royal tours a little, of getting rid of as much needless formality as possible and of really getting out among people and chatting in an easy and friendly way, they knew that here Princess Anne would be one of their assets.

She was very much the novice in regard to Royal tours, but she did not disappoint them. The Princess threw herself into the spirit of the casual, new approach. Perhaps it was not so difficult for her because she loves a challenge and is happier in an active rôle.

The walkabouts—as they came to be known from the Australian Aboriginal 'going walkabout', meaning to break away from the tribe and go off alone—began in Wellington, New Zealand, where Prince Charles joined the Royal party, and they continued in Australia.

They took place wherever and whenever the opportunity presented itself for the Royal party to step off the red carpet, and, splitting up, to dart off in different directions, to talk to people. From the beginning the walkabouts were a great success.

As they grew more successful they grew longer in time and distance. Sometimes the members of the Royal party were scattered over a quarter of a mile. Princess Anne, who will take a bicycle to the stables rather than walk a short distance, looked back one day with horror, and said: 'Do I have to walk back as far as that?'

But she entered into the spirit of the thing perfectly. She would charge into the waiting crowds as though she was joining friends she had known all her life. She would strike up a conversation that would gather in everyone within earshot.

People were delighted with her; she was transformed into a laughing girl with sparkling eyes. Transformed from what? Well, she had been thought a little dull up there on the dais. But then inactivity does that to Anne.

What she said may not have been all that remarkable. She wasn't furnishing quotable quotes, as her father and brother were—Prince Philip seeing a housewife clutching a paper shopping bag decorated with a reprint of the old poster, 'Wanted, Ned Kelly', grinned and called out 'Good heavens, are you still looking for him?'—but she was pleasant, pretty and warm.

Knowing her first big tour would be something of a strain for Anne, the Queen had decided that her daughter should not have a heavy programme of her own at first, that she would be eased gently into it.

The enthusiasms of Fiji, Tonga and New Zealand, where old loyalties are strong, had been very warming.

Left, *Birmingham Youth Festival, 1971*

Right, *Arriving at Ascot, 1973*

But Australia! Australia was different. Seven years before, the Queen and Prince Philip had made a tour of Australia that was undoubtedly something of a frost. They had tried to make it a new-style tour, driving around the suburbs on what became known as the 'milk run'. But that hadn't come off.

But in 1970 things went better. Prince Charles, having been to school for a short time in Australia, was readily acceptable. He had a good sense of humour, could use their slang—getting it right, not doing more harm than good by getting it half-right—and he spoke of Australia and Australians at all times with affection, although not at times without criticism.

But Princess Anne was given no quarter. Although she was accepted unquestionably by the old-guard Royalists, younger Australians thought she didn't measure up. Where was the swinging Princess, with the hallmark of King's Road, Chelsea, on her? Her clothes were too formal and gave no hint of those trendy boutiques flourishing in London. What about the girl who loved discos? Hadn't she danced on stage at 'Hair'? What was she doing now? The only evidence they had of her taste in music was when she jigged up and down when the band played 'Rule Britannia' and said in an aside to her father, 'our tune'. The only time she came home at dawn to the Royal yacht was after she had been visiting a school friend, not dancing the night away at a disco.

When she was seen dancing it was at a formal ball where she and Prince Charles were the guests of honour, a white-tie-and-tiara night. There was one less formal occasion, at Talbingo in the Snowy Mountains. There Princess Anne wore a trouser suit to a small party, slipped her shoes off and kicked as high as anyone at the finale of the rumbustious 'Snowy Mountains Roll'. But this, too, looked in the line of public duty, not the intimate glimpses of the Princess her peer group had been looking for.

If the Australian public showed their disappointment with the side of herself Princess Anne presented to them, for most of the time she hid her feelings about the reception she was given remarkably well for a girl of her spirit.

Her first chance to show what her attitude was when some University students asked her how she felt about the knockers.

She replied without a trace of anger or hurt: 'The knockers have to have someone. Once my father was the whipping post. Now it's me.'

Anne's dignity and directness stood her in good stead even when her programme became a rallying point for protest.

She has a stock reply to demands for support for causes outside her field, such as when she was questioned about the Australian Aborigines. 'What has it got to do with me?' she replied.

And she can twist the truth a little to get herself out of a tight spot. When asked by a student 'Do you work for your salary?' she replied 'My salary? I don't get one.' A half-truth because at that time she had an income on the Civil List of £15,000 as the daughter of the Sovereign.

Once when a group of students protesting against Anglo-Saxon imperialism dressed as druids and surrounded her while their leader shouted 'I am a direct descendant of Boadicea, the true queen,' the Princess gave them a look that would have done credit to Boadicea and shaken the Roman legions.

But sometimes it has got more desperate than that. She has been in the midst of unruly campus demonstrations, her visits have been threatened by boycott, she has arrived at universities to shouts of 'Clear off!' She had had sick jokes perpetrated on her such as a 'river of blood' spilled at her feet to draw attention to a lost cause. She had been mobbed by hooligan students, heckled by anti-royalists.

Whatever her feelings she keeps her equilibrium, even her sense of humour. After one particularly sticky encounter at a university, a moment later she was accepting with a smile a bunch of weeds from a student in drag who dropped a mock curtsey at her feet.

Father's girl

Although the Queen had to give her consent to the marriage of Princess Anne to Lieutenant Mark Phillips, Queen's Dragoon Guards, under the Royal Marriage Act of 1772, whereby no member of the Royal Family may contract matrimony without the consent of the Monarch, it was Prince Philip's permission the young subaltern sought first.

To Mark Phillips it was very important that Anne's father should approve of their being married. Though he confessed to being 'petrified' of Prince Philip, once he had come to the point he found him 'most helpful'. And of course Prince Philip was delighted that Anne and Mark, who had obviously fallen head over heels in love with each other, were anxious to announce their engagement.

For Anne's happiness is one of the most important things in Prince Philip's life; and he can deny her nothing.

Even on the day that Princess Anne was born nobody was in any doubt that she would be 'Daddy's Girl' from the moment he could lift her from the cradle. Prince Philip was then a young Lieutenant Commander waiting to take over his first ship, and probably it was the first time in his career he forgot his naval jargon: on the telephone to the King he described the new baby as 'the sweetest'. Not perhaps the sort of sugar-sweet description he would give nowadays, though he has never been less than delighted with his only daughter, who has remained close and become increasingly dear to him as time has passed.

Theirs has been a father/daughter relationship of a very special kind. Indeed, in an age when so many parents despair of communicating with their children once they begin to grow up, you could almost call it unique. Yet Prince Philip, who got busy with a broom sweeping away the cobwebs of outmoded tradition from Royalty, did, by the intelligent use of affection, preserve one of the finest ingredients of family life: the love and influence of a father. It was, in its way, rather beautifully old-fashioned.

Being Royal, father and daughter were never far from the public eye on weekends and on holiday, so it was soon noticed that he was no doting, overwhelmingly affectionate papa, nor Princess Anne the spoiled child. If anything, it was rather the other way round.

Prince Philip had to be very careful how he handled his daughter. She was born with all the characteristic Mountbatten temperament, and had their volatility and independence as well as a sharp intelligence the equal of his own. In so many ways, she was so like him. What she needed, if they were to avoid conflict, was not spoiling, but curbing.

The Princess responded quickly and eagerly to her father's teaching and leadership. As we have seen, she had a happy and unclouded childhood, and his only concern was that her natural affection for him did not become a fixation—a father fixation that could spoil her appreciation of the young men who would later play their parts in her life.

He needn't have worried: his careful handling of his daughter's affections was to be rewarded when she fell in love with a young man totally unlike her father.

The differences are many, one of the most obvious being that Mark Phillips is very far from the general conception of a father figure. Where Prince Philip served in the Navy, Mark is an Army man. Anne's father has always been trimly dressed, never in any way 'tweedy', while her future husband could definitely be described as 'county', riding to hounds—are in direct contrast to Prince Philip, who abhors all blood sports. Conversely, Mark is a champion equestrian, with a strong love for horses, while Prince Philip, as a polo player, has always been hard on his ponies. To conclude the list, Lieutenant Phillips is a man of few words, in the military fashion, happier firing tank guns while Prince Philip fires his famous verbal broadsides.

Prince Philip had a pillar-to-post childhood, so much younger than his four sisters, who were by the time he was born already married to German aristocrats. His father, Prince Andrew of Greece, lived in exile, while his mother, Princess Alice, was already a recluse. After he married, with children of his own, he liked to keep closely in touch with the rest of his family. With him the Princess paid flying visits to Leichtenstein and Germany, meeting her aunts and cousins. When she became engaged she flew straight to Germany to show off both Mark and the ring to no less than three aunts and twenty-seven cousins at family celebration gatherings.

Prince Philip has spent a lot of time with Anne encouraging her in her outdoor activites. On the ski slopes close to his sister's castles he watched her take her first tumble in the snow. He taught her to swim in the pool at Buckingham Palace—she could dive from his shoulders by the time she was six. At the age of eight, seated in his lap in the Lagonda, she mastered the art of driving, and by the time she was nine she could drive a bubble car alone on the private roads around Windsor.

He taught her to sail and she crewed for him. At barbecues he let her do the cooking, though she confessed that she only liked this 'provided my father is there to tell me what to do'. Whenever he played polo at Windsor the Princess groomed his ponies.

One of the nicest things he did for the Princess was to see that she was dressed sensibly, like other little girls. It

110

was about the time that he was modernising Buckingham Palace with intercoms, tape recorders, mimeographs for the archives, coloured flags pinpointing Royal movements on wall maps, and a helicopter on the lawn. In keeping with these improvements, he came to the conclusion that he was not going to have his tomboy daughter dressed in fussy effeminate clothes.

Though the Queen and Prince Philip have always moved with the times—and by now they were changing fast—the public image of Royalty, by its tradition, moves just that much slower. The image of a fairy-tale Princess who lived in a fairy-tale Palace was still cherished. If Princess Anne did not fit naturally into this sort of rosy picture her father could not see any reason why she should be made to do so.

She was outgrowing smocked dresses, frilly bonnets, fur muff and chain—the all-dressed-up-for-a-party look which traditionally had been the stamp of a Princess. He could not for the life of him see why the Princess should not wear the kind of tough, comfortable clothes the kids in the suburbs were wearing. The Queen fortunately agreed, and bought her daughter dungarees and bright jerseys, windcheaters and later a Beatles cap, the logical climax to the kind of casual clothes that Princess Anne has always been happy wearing.

As she grew up, orders and decorations, a family tiara and heirloom jewels were to show her rank of Royalty clearly enough when the occasion demanded. So there was never any reason to complain that casual clothes could be too great a leveller. And the occasions

112

for wearing them were hardly ones that could make the situation arise very often: riding, polo and yachting are scarcely the pastimes of the masses.

It must have been a great help to the young Princess, who did not escape the normal little jealousies of a younger sister, to have a father who spent so much time making sure that her life was a full and happy one. Princess Anne herself has spoken about the times when she was offended, in that deep way that children are, as her elder brother went off and she was left feeling very much out of things.

On the day of the Queen's Coronation, just twenty years before she and Mark announced their engagement, the Princess was left behind at Buckingham Palace while Charles was taken to Westminster Abbey by his grandmother, Queen Elizabeth the Queen Mother. In later years Anne was to recall: 'I was *full* of sisterly fury at being left behind.'

It was obvious that Prince Charles was perfectly qualified to be the 'favourite', with his boyish good looks, his politeness and his appealing shyness. Such a contrast to Anne's famous tantrums! But the Queen had strong emotions against favouritism, and punctiliously made no difference between the children. The Queen Mother, however, made no secret of the fact that she adored the little Prince Charles.

On the Queen Mother's sixtieth birthday a luncheon was given by Princess Margaret in her first married home, and invitations were issued to every member of the Royal Family. Prince Charles was allowed a day off from his prep school. Afterwards he told Anne, sparing no little sister's feelings: 'It was supah.' She was on the verge of tears.

As some token of consolation Prince Philip took her to another of the Commonwealth cocktail parties. If nothing else, it certainly smoothed ruffled feelings.

Little twinges of jealously would occasionally be aired in public, as when the Royal children were helping out at a sale of work in Braemar. From time to time Anne would make forays from her own stand towards her brother's. 'She's pinching all my customers!' he called out in exasperation as Anne yet again pulled a few prospective clients away to buy some of her paper serviettes.

'I'm selling more than Charles,' she announced triumphantly.

Mademoiselle Bibiane de Rougoux, who spent a summer in Balmoral to tutor the children in French, found them 'real little devils'. They were forever sparring, and on the moors around the beautifully set castle in the north east of Scotland there was no way of stopping their childish warfare. 'They were always arguing who should have the honour of retrieving the grouse.'

But of course, as children will, they eventually grew beyond the stage of petty jealousies. In their formative years, however, Prince Philip kept a watchful eye on the Princess until she was old enough to understand her position in the family vis-a-vis an elder brother who would one day become the King of England. As the

Queen said: 'Anne takes things so much better from her father.'

When Prince Charles went into first the Royal Air Force, then later the Royal Navy, Princess Anne unhesitatingly accepted a heavier official programme to assist the Queen and leave him free—though nobody could refer to it as freedom if they were within earshot of the Princess.

'What do you mean—freedom?' she snapped back when one well-meaning person ventured to suggest that her elder brother might be enjoying his comparative escape from responsibility.

Prince Charles used to share with his sister a sitting room adjoining their suites in Buckingham Palace. With their two younger brothers they liked to keep together as a family during holidays. Gradually, however, the gap between Charles' interests and Anne's began to

Chiengmai, Thailand, February 1971

widen, and eventually the days started to drag. Anne, with the frankness that she is so well known for, summed up the situation exactly when she said: 'By the time the holidays were over we had had enough of each other. We could say goodbye cheerfully, if a little thankfully.'

How love and marriage were to change all that. When Princess Anne was all set to go off to a life of her own with Mark Phillips she could hardly have been more delighted to see her elder brother around. He flew home from the Caribbean specially to take part in the engagement celebrations.

At a time when most average teenagers are tending to throw off their parental ties, Princess Anne could hardly conceal her joy at the prospect of going with her father to Jamaica and the Commonwealth Games, where they were joined by Prince Charles. He had flown from his school in Australia, Timbertop, which in later years he was to show her round, and she was fascinated with all the stories he had of his school life there and the Australian slang that he had somehow picked up.

The days at the games, seated close to Prince Philip, could hardly fail to be exciting, as athletics were a new dimension in sport for the Princess. It was an interest that she would never lose: her future husband, Mark Phillips, is himself no mean athlete, whose record of 14 ft. 9 in. for the long jump still stands at his prep school, Stouts Hill, and who was captain of athletics during his final year at his public school, Marlborough.

In Kingston, at the ball which followed the close of

the Games, the Princess danced with some of the athletes, not with any spurious liveliness because it was a duty, but because as a girl of almost sixteen she was really beginning to see and enjoy a bit of life.

Neither Princess Anne nor, indeed, anyone else concerned with Royal tradition, thought it strange that she should be brought into public life by her father. In another day and age, of course, it would have been more suitable for her to have been brought out by her mother.

The Queen, as Princess Elizabeth, and Princess Margaret had their first experience of Royal duties when they were accompanied by the late King George VI and Queen Elizabeth, now the Queen Mother, on the Royal Tour of South Africa in 1947. Princess Alexandra was taken on a tour of Canada by her mother, then the Duchess of Kent, to initiate her into Royal duties. In fact Royal Princesses, right back to the girl who was to become Queen Mary, spent the whole of their early lives in public supported in their major rôles by elder ladies of the Royal family.

It was perhaps just as well that Princess Anne was something of a tomboy and never overly concerned about her appearance, for otherwise that first big occasion might have been little short of a disaster. No sooner had the trip to Jamaica been arranged than the Princess fell off her horse and broke her nose.

For many girls of her age it would have been an accident close to tragedy: even the slightest skin blemish can send adolescent girls rushing nervously to the mirror. But Princess Anne was made of a different cloth. Even after the operation to reset her nose had been performed she seemed to be totally unworried about its shape.

Not so her closest observers, who promptly put her under the most minute scrutiny. 'Had the plastic surgeons done a better job for her than nature?' came the questions.

'To bob or not to bob' was an inner debate that exercised the minds of many TV stars and personalities facing the expanding new medium. But plastic surgery got no boost from the Princess's nose. The Royal nose was seen to have a distinct family likeness and lacked none of her character.

That visit to Jamaica was almost certainly a turning point in the life of the young Princess, soon to have to make up her mind on the weighty question of what she

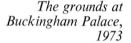

The grounds at Buckingham Palace, 1973

should make of her career. She would, of course, toe the Royal line—'but,' she clearly decided, 'in father's way.'

For her there could be no other.

She was to make her mark in the same way that her father had done, to know criticism as he had, and to sacrifice popularity for the sake of retaining her own individuality. On the other hand, there was no shortage of popular acclaim to carry her on wave after wave of adulation.

But it was the criticism, lacking the gentleness that would have been necessary in an earlier age, that was to crystallize her feelings for her father. While she was growing up he had been her champion so, naturally enough, now she would become his. When, in 1970, the tide of popularity was to turn against her she identified with Prince Philip straight away:

'There are always people waiting for me to put my foot in it. Just like my father,' she said to a group of people at a public gathering. As she spoke, Princess Anne struck one of her more awkward attitudes, legs at an angle, hands behind her back, head tilted to one side. About her whole stance there was a challenging look, almost a defiant one.

Later, when criticism was again levelled at her, she restated her feelings, as we have heard, in no uncertain terms. 'So', she said, 'The knockers have to have some-one. Once my father was the whipping post. Now it's me.'

At that moment the mantle of Prince Philip, that

strange mixture of charisma and bluntness, seemed to devolve gently on her young shoulders.

But not all the gentlemen of the Press found Anne's strength of character upsetting. Indeed one journalist, paying tribute to her acceptance of the rôle, declared proudly in bold headlines: 'I'm an Anne's Man.'

It is unlikely that Prince Philip and Princess Anne set out deliberately to create this father-and-daughter image, but the conception of this ideal relationship caught on. So that the head of a dynasty, or a republic, or a member of their own Commonwealth would invite the two of them together 'for the pleasure of their company'. Here both Prince Philip's and Princess Anne's position in relation to the sovereign is very clearly defined. Where a visit from the Queen is very much a State occasion, a visit from her consort and her daughter is very much less official.

They were invited together to the Shah of Persia's great anniversary celebrations, when a whole city under canvas was set up in the desert beside the ruins of Persepolis. The celebrations themselves were an extravaganza on which the Shah lavished a small fortune. The luxury tents in which the guests lived were spread around beautiful gardens and refreshingly cool swimming pools. The canvas was the colour of the desert sand, the tents hung inside with rich brocade, the floors covered with priceless Persian carpets. The food and entertainment were supplied on the same magnanimous scale. Chefs were flown in specially for the occasion from Paris—indeed, the famous Maxim's had to close down for three days while their staff assisted in the Shah's celebrations in Iran. Every known delicacy was served up for the delight of the guests, from stuffed peacocks in the land of the Peacock Throne to Royal sturgeon in aspic, and caviar from the Caspian Sea.

The Princess brought with her a superb wardrobe of clothes to wear during the festivities. She and her father made a most handsome couple and were the subject of considerable admiration on the part of the cream of European Society, heads of State, the 'International Set' and younger members of Europe's other Royal families. The Shah and Queen Farah Dibah later told how they found Anne enchanting 'with her coolness and touch of pensiveness'.

An American diplomat's wife summed up her own opinion of the Princess: 'She looks so well bred and not a bit horsey; slightly aloof with a hint of arrogance. Just what we expected. A typical Englishwoman of her class.'

But this is only one side of Princess Anne: the other is an outdoor girl. She has spent nearly every birthday she can remember at sea with her father, either on board *Britannia* or sailing the yawl *Bloodhound*.

Her birthday falls during the holidays when the Royal Family go to Balmoral, scene of so many birthday parties and balls: both the Queen Mother and Princess Margaret have their birthdays in August. Yet Princess Anne has never had a birthday party there: even the

Father's girl

party for her twenty-first birthday was on board *Britannia*, when she jumped the gun and had the party a little earlier while the royal yacht was in Cowes.

Before Anne met Mark she would never pass up the chance to celebrate by quietly cruising around the Western Isles of Scotland with Prince Philip. Sometimes they would be utterly alone on the yawl except for a small crew loaned from *Britannia*. They would explore the lochs and inlets, tie up and go ashore for picnics, cruising around some of the most beautiful scenery in the world, from Loch Fyne to the Caledonian Canal.

Anne will probably never forget her nineteenth birthday, which she spent with her father and Prince Charles sailing up and down the Norwegian fiords. It was to be

The garden of Government House, Singapore, February 1972

the last cruise on the yawl *Bloodhound*, which was sold later in the same year.

Personal Appearance

If you want to make Princess Anne annoyed try suggesting that she needs to diet to keep her slim athletic figure. The Princess will quickly defend herself. Once, for example, the wife of a young man who had been in the Royal entourage on one of the Princess's tours, mentioned that she had read with interest in a magazine an article about the diet the Princess used.

The Princess let fly with a sustained attack on the magazine which had printed the article. 'Don't mention that paper to me,' she flashed back angrily. 'I'm furious with them, publishing a diet I'm supposed to be on. I am *not* on a diet.'

Princess Anne was speaking the truth. Like many active sports people, she does not have to go on diets. Unlike Mark, she does not have to resort to any of the

Princess Anne

more drastic measures; like taking pills, appetite sup-
pressors, or sweating off extra pounds.

An ex-girl friend of Mark's wrote that at the beginning of every year he had to begin the battle to reduce
his 6 ft. $1\frac{1}{2}$ in. frame from $12\frac{3}{4}$ stone to $11\frac{3}{4}$ stone for competitive riding. Mark would admit to this, but point out
the dangers of heavy dieting: 'You have to be careful.
Three hours in a Turkish bath loses you 7 pounds, but
you could easily flake out in a cross-country run.'

Princess Anne, however, does not have any of these
problems, she keeps her good figure by what she calls
'just sensible eating'.

Developing the habit of eating sensibly was no easier
for Princess Anne than any other girl. For example, she
used to enjoy a refreshing glass of coke but this, along
with other foods like sugar and potatoes, she was
encouraged to give up.

Left, *Anne at
Buckingham Palace,
1973*

Right, *The People's
Palace, Khartoum,
Sudan, 1973*

Instead she was advised to eat heartily but on a heavy protein diet, which included plenty of meat, fish, poultry (expecially poultry), lots of pure lemon juice (instead of coke), salads and green vegetables. Also she was not allowed to finish off the meal with any tasty extras like sweets, cheese or even fruit, and her liquid intake was restricted to four cupfuls a day.

Obviously, there must have been many moments when an active young girl like the Princess must have been tempted on a hot sunny afternoon to treat herself to just one glass of her favourite coke, or perhaps just one cream cake, to stave off hunger between meals.

The Queen herself helped Anne enormously to establish this new pattern of eating. Following a similar diet herself since her marriage has helped her remain slim, smart and youthful-looking ever since, and yet also fulfil a heavy programme which needs all her energy.

In time, however, the Princess through trial and error developed an eating pattern which helped her to develop into the elegant figure we see today.

There would have been times when she must have got very discouraged while developing this pattern of eating, as it required her testing herself with all the foods she liked to eat. This meant that for three days she would eat a food not generally included in her usual diet, like cakes, cheese or a helping of marmalade. After three days it was necessary for her to weigh in and check, and if there was no weight increase, she then knew that that particular food could be enjoyed all the time.

The result is that the Princess knows exactly what she

can or can't eat in order to retain her most enviable figure. She is a good 5 ft. 6¼ in. tall with a high and pretty rounded bust, a neat 24 in waist, which she makes the most of by often wearing tightly fitting waisted dresses. Perhaps also one of her best assets is her long shapely legs, which help her to look so elegant in the trousers suits she is often seen in.

As everyone knows, a sensible diet can also help

1971 Badminton Horse Trials

retain a good complexion, and the Princess has been fortunate in inheriting the Royal family's smooth milky complexion. She has learnt how to make the most of this for both her everyday duties as well as the more formal functions she has to attend.

Princess Anne learnt the expertise of make-up from a leading beautician, although she did learn the art of good grooming while still at school.

For evening or when she has to face up to the arc light, she uses a heavier make-up. She has made two television films for the Save the Children Fund, of which she is President, and although this called for a special technique in make-up she was able to apply most of it herself with very little help from experts.

She is also adept at using only the very slightest touch of cosmetics during the day to keep a natural look. When she is riding she wears little or no make-up, but as she is out in all weathers she believes in using a good nourishing cream as part of her beauty routine.

Just as she looks after her good figure by eating sensibly, and has no need to resort to drastic diets, so she looks after her young and healthy complexion and has no need for beauty aids like facials or face packs.

Princess Anne has had, from her teenage days, something approaching an obsession with her hair. Her hair is thick, strong and long, but it is also very crinkly, and in consequence can be extremely difficult to manage. She says herself, 'It is my life's work taming it.'

She has, however, learnt to tame it very well. Going to

school at Benenden helped her greatly, as she, like all the other girls there, had to do her own hair all of the time. She learnt not only hair care, but how to give herself a shampoo and set.

For school, she turned her mop of unruly curls into a neat page boy style, but watching what other girls of her own age were doing with their hair, and Anne's constant anxiety to be abreast of fashion, led to some behind the scene tussles at the Palace. For example, once, in her usual stubborn manner, she insisted on wearing a white stretchy hair band to an important evening function. It was thought by the Palace officials to be not quite suitable for the occasion, but her picture taken there must have delighted every other teenager.

After she left school she shocked the Court hairdresser, who had regularly attended at court for four generations, by washing her own hair. No other Royal lady in his recollection had ever put her head down in a washbasin and dried it off herself.

Learning how to handle her own hair, however, was an invaluable part of the Princess's training, particularly when she took up her official duties, which meant a good deal of travelling and to some very out of the way places. Like 'Talbarea', a sheep station in Queensland where the Princess managed to go riding in the morning, muster sheep, spend the afternoon swimming and still look very pretty at a dance in the evening with a smart new hairdo.

The Princess has always had a good sense of style, which quickly developed when she came into public life.

She recognised what a disaster a dowdy hair-do can make of anyone's appearance, and became very adept at evolving new hair styles, and creating some very pretty ones with the help of hair pieces. At one time she had twenty-two of these, the fashion writers calculated, as well as other modern beauty equipment like large hot rollers, hand dryers and electric tongs. She never travels without these and uses them to straighten her wild curly hair into a smooth flow at the end of a day in the open, or to create something more exotic for formal occasions.

For some years the Princess shared the Queen's hairdresser, but often found this inconvenient. For example when they were travelling on board the *Britannia* on their Royal tours, she would have to wait until her mother's hair was done in the evening before hers could be started on, and for this reason she was very thankful she could manage on her own.

Princess Anne now has her own hairdresser. For her twenty-first birthday pictures, which were released officially, her hair was done by a new hairdresser and she was so pleased with the results that she settled for him to do her hair from that time on.

This was Michael, one half of the firm Michael John, who now sometimes attends the Princess in her personal suite where she has all the equipment a hairdresser needs, from a back-wash to a standing hair dryer. The appointment is usually around six o'clock in the evening.

At other times the Princess will go to the Salon where there is a private room downstairs for V.I.Ps. Often she

134

has her hair done two or three times a week, but one appointment at least she likes to keep when she has a special hair treatment to keep it in good condition. Hair care was another lesson drilled into her at school as one of the secrets of good grooming.

Michael is one of London's leading hair stylists, and works closely with the glossy fashion magazines, projecting the newest fashion images in hairstyles. His clientelle, naturally, tend to be models, film stars and women whose public appearance is very important.

The Princess leads a very full life and it would be impossible for her to depend on her hairdresser all of the time, so it is still necessary for her to handle her own hair for a lot of important functions, especially after a day training her horses or racing.

It has been suggested that the Princess might find it easier to manage her hair if she had it cut short. How ever, she was appalled at the idea and said, 'I like long hair, and I am quite prepared to take the extra trouble to keep it looking as well as I can. Short hair,' she added, 'bored her.'

It is as important to the Princess psychologically, as it is to most women young or old, to feel that her hair looks nice.

The Princess nearly always has to wear a hat at official occasions; riding hats when she is training her horses or competing, and for the more formal functions a band box appearance is required of her.

John Boyd, a charming, soft spoken Scot, makes all

the Princess's hats. 'Considering the Princess hates hats she wears them well,' he says. She likes to go into his shop and try them all on.

It would be impossible for the Princess to take enough different hats with her to match all the different outfits she wears on official tours. Instead she takes one with a sweeping brim and gives it many lives by swathing a piece of fabric round it, to match whatever she is wearing at the time. This is a fashion trick that has been frequently copied.

For example she changed the look of her generation when she wore a white stetson hat around which she would tie the long flowing scarves. Through her imagination and flair she has brought hats back into fashion for the young, and the trendy shops in Kings Road, Chelsea, are now copying her.

The Princess tries with all her clothes to buy garments that will serve as many purposes as possible. 'Clothes are just part of my job,' she says, and she has never considered herself as a trend setter, but rather believes that her fashion image is on the whole fairly staid.

There are however, few people who would go along with that.

Her bright personality is reflected in her fashion sense. She likes bright colours and large patterns, clothes which are vivid and eye-catching. She prefers to shop around for her clothes, dropping into boutiques, buying trendy clothes off the peg.

Unlike most members of the Royal family she does not like to have clothes specially made for her. She considers the problems of choosing a style from half a dozen sketches, and then finding a suitable kind of material for that particular style, plus the long fitting sessions, to be boring and time consuming, especially when the end result is often not quite what she wanted.

With ready-made clothes, however, she can try them on and if they don't feel right, there are always plenty of others waiting to be tried on. Also the Princess is fortunate in having a good figure, and can easily step into a dress without any alterations having to be made.

Princess Anne buys a lot of her clothes from Susan Smalls, the ready-to-wear firm. Maureen Baker, the designer there, says, 'She has very definite ideas of her own.' This firm has also been honoured with the order to make Princess Anne's dress for her wedding at Westminster Abbey. Maureen Baker says she couldn't believe it when the Princess just casually mentioned that she wanted her to make the wedding dress. 'I was dumbfounded', she added emphatically.

It was typical of Princess Anne to break with tradition and not go to the Royal couturier. She did what so many of her own generation would do. She asked the girl who had made so many of her favourite dresses to design something special for the day. The fifteen girls working on the wedding dress each sewed a snip of their hair into the hem—for luck.

Princess Anne has also had many of her glamorous dresses from John Langberg, of Christian Dior (London). There also she digs through the clothes rack, wasting no time in choosing what she wants. 'We do not

even have to have a special room for her to try the dress on', said John Langberg of the Princess.

There are many other top names in fashion who have had the honour of dressing the Princess. These famous names include Gina Fratina, who dressed the Princess for one of those special twenty-first birthday pictures, and we have seen the Princess in bridesmaids dresses by Bellville and Sassoon. Lastly, many of the elegant coats we see the Princess wearing and looking so smart in, are supplied for her by Louis Feraud. Wherever she goes to buy her clothes she is liked, not only as a Royal patron, but because she is always so pleasant to serve. She is never any trouble as she knows exactly what she wants, and exactly what suits her, not requiring any special attention.

Just as the Princess has been allowed freedom in many ways — unlike members of the Royal Family in past generations — the Queen gave her daughter the freedom to choose her own clothes. Thus the Princess has chosen her clothes since the age of sixteen and, like all girls, *has* made mistakes.

Once, for an official birthday picture, she bought from a leading store a dress designed by a bridal wear firm for the bride's mother. As photographs subsequently showed it was not suitable for a sixteen-year-old girl. But as the late and elegant Princess Marina pointed out to the Queen: 'There is no other way to teach them except by their own mistakes.'

Princess Anne has learnt her lessons well. This experience together with her strength of character, has

142

given Anne the courage to break conventions in her dress so that she has grown up into an elegant young women whose clothes show not only individuality of styles but a flair for fashion which has made her a recognised trend setter in clothes for her generation.

The future for
Anne and Mark

'They could almost have been computer-dated,' said the
Queen Mother, who can always be depended on for a
crisp and up-to-date judgment on family matters, when
Princess Anne and Mark Phillips became engaged.
Who can doubt after her own happy marriage that the
Queen Mother was thinking in terms of mutual love,
character and common interests? She herself had been a
non-Royal bride although a member of the aristocracy
and she had seen many changes since then. She had said
on the day of Princess Margaret's engagement to the
talented young photographer Antony Armstrong-Jones:
'They were made for each other.'

But why would Mark Phillips seem so suitable to the
Royal family, for a Princess who might have made any

145

choice she wished? Neither Mark Phillips nor anyone of his type was ever on the lists of European ex-royalty or royalty, or of suitable sprigs of the English aristocracy, which were regularly compiled for the benefit of Princess Anne.

The overriding family reason is, of course, that Anne and Mark are seriously in love. The reason which most affects the monarchy itself is that the Queen and her advisers know that the overwhelming number of her people would prefer a Britisher to a foreigner. And after the marriages of Princess Margaret and Princess Alexandra have shown that marriage with a commoner these days presents no great practical difficulties to a Princess, they are just as happy if the bridegroom is not a member of the aristocracy. Anne's choice fits the temper of the times and the Monarchy never for a moment neglects to study the temper of the times.

Apart from his personal qualities, two things about Mark Phillips naturally appeal strongly to the Royal family: his choice of career and his love of horses. The Royal family still believes in service careers so strongly that Prince Charles has had spells in two of the services. Here the Royal family is in tune with the British people, most of whom think that a spell of service to one's country is a good start in life for a young man even if in these days it doesn't so often become a lifetime career.

But Mark Phillips' love of horses had placed him in a very different set of people from Royal circles. And it was into these circles that he introduced Anne.

Horsey people, or the hunting set, are popularly

regarded as what used to be called 'fast'. They tend—
and here Anne and Mark fit perfectly into the pattern—
to be people who put great emphasis on physical skills,
their horsemanship, probably fast cars and so on. It is
said that they work hard, play hard and sometimes drink
hard and play around.

There is no doubt, and this is inevitable because of
the generation that separates them, that Princess Anne
would not be as touchingly ingenuous as her mother, the
Queen, who was near tears when she first realised that
divorce could come as close to her as her personal
friends. Often, one can imagine, Princess Anne would
have raised an eyebrow or turned a shoulder from
behaviour that certainly still wouldn't be accepted in
Royal circles.

But the abiding interest of the young lovers was the
horses themselves. And Mark Phillips, on the evidence
of his courtship and proposal, is an engagingly old-
fashioned young man. Added to this is the certainty that
Princess Anne remains always conscious of her Royal
position—although not often in the foot-stamping,
imperious way that sometimes characterised Princess
Margaret—and as well is an extremely commonsensical
and fastidious young woman.

But even given their love and the warmth and support
of both their families, Anne and Mark will face many
hurdles in the future.

Mark has already implied that marrying Anne doesn't
necessarily mean giving up his Army career. But it will

The Vale of Leven
Industrial Estate,
Dumbarton, July 1971

mean losing some of his freedom and having to share a good deal of the limelight that constantly focuses on Royalty.

'Obviously I gave a great deal of thought to the loss of privacy before going into this,' he recalled as his regiment celebrated his engagement.

Much will depend on Mark's character, and already he has sometimes been a good counter to Anne's volatility.

People who knew him as a child say he was a rather shy little boy who has grown up a pleasant person with a quiet unruffled charm.

During the courtship, while Princess Anne was likely to lose her temper and let fly at the pursuing press, Lieutenant Phillips was quiet and more subtle. Later he confessed: 'When two people are in love and want to be together they find ways and means.'

And it was he who found the ways and means.

Their courtship is full of indications of how quietly, placidly Mark Phillips takes the lead.

Since the days of Queen Victoria there has been a persistent belief that a Royal Princess makes the running when it comes to the matrimonial stakes. There is not much to support this in recent generations. But on the other hand Princess Anne's character suggests that she would not only do what she wanted in life and get what she wanted.

But when it came to love, did she pursue Mark? He says no. And is horrified at reports that she proposed to him. 'I know of no protocol that says it has to be done that way,' he defended himself at the very thought. And while he says he did not exactly go down on his knees to Princess Anne to ask her to marry him he says: 'I did propose to her.'

From the moment of their engagement a good deal of gratuitous advice on how to handle Anne was handed out to Mark.

And there were many who took a distinctly sour view of the future of the young lovers. 'I can't imagine any good-looking young man like Mark Phillips giving up the promise of a carefree, cushioned life for a marriage that could well turn out to be tough going,' said a woman who knows them both.

Another acquaintance's view was: 'I imagine it will be one of those tempestuous, tea-cup throwing marriages which survive on the well known and often satisfactory pattern of violent storms and then glorious moments of kiss-and-make-up.'

This sort of view is rejected by the people who know them best, and, more importantly, the people who have seen both Anne and Mark at moments of great personal stress. 'People don't know what they are talking about,' a member of the British Horse Society said indignantly, then added: 'Mark can handle the Queen's horse Columbus with his streak of cussedness,' implying that hence Mark could handle anything.

'Princess Anne and Mark have this love of horses. It brought them together. It will keep them together,' said a Master of Foxhounds, who at one time lent Princess

Princess Anne at the
official Government
Reception, Belgrade,
October 1972

Princess Anne on
the Isle of Sark
May 1972

Anne a horse when she took up the chase. 'We think their future is not only enviable but their love indestructible.'

'Mark's future?' queried a high Army officer. 'He can handle that. No trouble at all. He was born a gentleman and has had all the training in the world as a sportsman and a soldier.'

But all the confidence and good wishes in the world cannot make the future of Anne and Mark as simple as other people's marriages. When Mark says 'I hope I will make all the decisions for all the important things,' he is speaking like every old-fashioned, young bridegroom. For this cannot be. After marriage Princess Anne will remain a Royal princess. The Queen and Prince Philip will do everything they can to help her build a happy and serene family life but they cannot give her a future duty-free or care-free. With their own strong sense of duty and obligation they would not wish it for her, and she would not wish it for herself. Therefore, Anne will continue to fulfil the role that has won her the love and admiration of the British people. In the way that Princess Alexandra and Princess Margaret have successfully combined their public lives with happy and normal homes; undoubtedly, with the support and understanding of Mark Phillips, Princess Anne will achieve the same harmony and balance.

Some of the important decisions for Anne and Mark will be made by the Royal family, out of their sense of public obligation; some may be made by the British

Government; some may be made by changing events. But fulfilling their obligations in life will not cloud the future for young people such as Princess Anne and Mark Phillips.

And when Mark says of their future: 'She will be my wife,' he knows what he means, Anne knows what he means. And both are content.

Printed and bound in Britain by W. S. Cowell Ltd,
Ipswich on Hi-Speed cartridge paper made by
Wiggins-Teape, and supplied by Frank Grunfeld Ltd.